Introduction

This series of books provides a foundation for a five-year course in Religious Education for pupils aged eleven to sixteen. Each book contains fifty units of work, each of which forms the basis of one lesson or period. The course follows a thematic approach to the study of major world religions found in Britain today — Christianity, Judaism, Islam, Hinduism, Buddhism and Sikhism. The approach is open-ended and questioning, and assumes no particular religious stance on the part of the reader.

ILLUSTRATIONS AND TEXT

The illustrations are an integral part of the course, and the text is closely related to the illustrations. It is suggested that the teacher should make use of the details of the illustrations as an expansion and clarification of the text. The text is deliberately brief and simple; wherever difficult religious words or concepts are introduced, they are emphasised and explained.

Many pupils will be able to go on to further reading. Suggestions for suitable books are listed in the Bibliography.

DISCUSSION QUESTIONS

It is essential that young people should be given the opportunity to think out for themselves the religious issues raised by the text: the purpose of human life, the problem of suffering and evil, the possibility of life after death, the existence of God. The discussion questions given in each unit provide starters for such discussion. They are not comprehension questions, and although the text provides some answers, many of the questions do not have conclusive agreed answers.

The discussion questions will generally lend themselves to discussion in small groups, followed by class discussion and individual written work.

THINGS TO DO

After each section, suggestions are offered for further activities involving visits, talks, modelling, drawing, and imaginative written work. The use of audio-visual aids, libraries, reference books and artefacts should enable all schools, however remote their setting, to tackle most of the suggested activities.

I am most grateful to the following people, who have read all or part of the manuscript of this book and made many helpful comments and suggestions:

Rabbi Douglas Charing, Riadh El-Droubie, Mick Guha, Robin Shepherd, Dalfit Singh, Sardar A. K. Singh, Peter Woodward, Mrs Nina Taylor, and Susanne, my wife.

John Bailey

Acknowledgements

The author and the publishers wish to thank the following for permission to use copyright material:

Picturepoint Ltd.: pp. 8, 17, 32 (top), 40, 66, 80, 82, 83, 95, 100
The British Library: pp. 10, 14, 18, 32, 101 (also on cover), 102, 121
Camerapix Hutchison: pp. 11 (McIntyre), 15 (Lister), 23 (top, McIntyre), 24 (Pate), 25 (Goycolea), 29 (Goycolea), 34 (Griffiths-Jones), 35 (Montagnon), 36 (Errington), 96, 99 (Scorer)
Ann and Bury Peerless, Slide Resources & Picture Library: pp. 12, 13, 16, 19, 20, 22, 23, 26, 27, 38, 42, 106, 108, 110, 111, 112, 114 (foot), 116, 118, 120, 122
Rev. J. Catling Allen: pp. 44, 53, 71, 103
The Shrine of the Book, Israel Museum, Jerusalem: p. 45
Joachim Blauel – Artothek: p. 48
Sonia Halliday Photographs: p. 50, 54 (left)
Vatican Museums: pp. 52, 56
Pfarrer Werner Schnell: p. 54 (right)
Museo del Prado, Madrid: p. 57
National Gallery of Art, Washington: pp. 58 (Ailsa Mellon Bruce Fund 1965), 72 (Samuel H. Kress Collection 1961), 84 (Widener Collection 1942)
Tyne and Wear County Council Museums: p. 59 (from the collection at Sunderland Museum and Art Gallery)
Jewish Education Bureau: p. 60
Itzchak Genut, 28 Harav Hertzog Street, Givataim, Israel: pp. 46, 61, 62 (from the Rothschild Collection), 63, 64, 65, 67, 68
Kunsthistorische Museum, Wien: p. 70
Jamie Simson/DAS Photo: p. 73
The Trustees of the National Gallery, London: p. 74
The Frick Collection, New York: p. 76
Scala/Firenze: p. 78
Photo Giraudon. Musée d'Unterlinden, Colmar: p. 81
John Rylands University Library of Manchester: p. 85
Bodleian Library, Oxford: pp. 86 (MS.Can.Bibl.Lat.62,f.1ᵛ), 88 (Douce Bible Eng. 1583b.), 90 (MS.Bodley 264,f.223), 91 (MS.Digby 227,f.13)
The Board of Trustees of the Victoria and Albert Museum: p. 92
The Islamic Foundation, Leicester: pp. 94, 98
Sardar A. K. Singh: p. 114 (top)

Contents

Hinduism

Many religions of the world are named after their founders, and date from the time when the founder lived. The Western calendar, for example, takes as its starting-point the birth of Jesus Christ, and dates are given as A.D. (Anno Domini, meaning "Year of our Lord"), C.E. (Christian, or Common, Era), and B.C. or B.C.E. for dates before the birth of Jesus Christ.

Hinduism is different from the general rule. The name Hindu comes from the Persian word Sindhu, meaning river. This is how the great Indus river, which flows through north-west India, gets its name. The Persians called India "the land beyond the Sindhu", and this led to its inhabitants coming to be known as Hindus. As their way of life and their religion could not be separated, the religion eventually came to be known as Hinduism.

Unlike other religions, Hinduism had no founder. We cannot look back to any one historical figure, or even group, through whom Hinduism could be said to have begun. This section deals with the historical origins of Hinduism, and the ancient books of Hindu scripture in which the basic beliefs of Hinduism may be found.

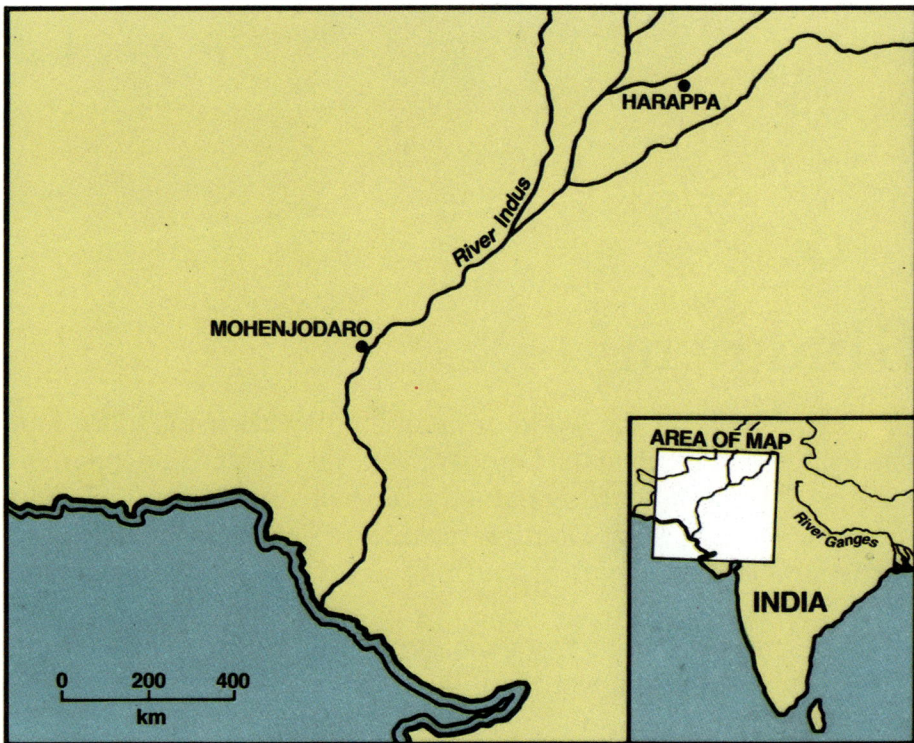

The Indus valley

Wheels of the sun god's chariot at the Temple of Surya, Konarak

1 The Origins of Hinduism

Four thousand years ago, many different tribes of people lived in India. In the Indus valley, a great civilisation had grown up, and archaeologists have recently found much evidence of this civilisation in the excavations at Harappa and Mohenjodaro.

About 1500 B.C.E., India was invaded from the north-west by people from central Asia who called themselves *Aryans* (Nobles). They were tall, light-skinned warriors who overran the peoples living in the Indus valley. The Aryans were nomads, but they gradually settled in villages and became farmers. As the invaders took control, a rigid class system developed. This is called the *caste* system (from the Portuguese word *casta*, meaning race). Originally, the top caste was the *kshatriyas*, or warrior-rulers (the Aryan invaders). As Hindu society evolved, however, the *brahmins* (priests) became more and more important, until they became the top caste.

Early Hinduism was a form of nature worship. The forces of nature — fire, storm and sun — were worshipped as gods. The most important god of the Aryan invaders was Indra, god of both storm and war. There are 250 hymns to Indra in the collection of ancient writings called the *Rig Veda*. Another early god was Varuna, the sky god. He was thought to control the days and nights, and the seasons of the year, and so became the upholder of order in the universe. The sun god, Savitar, was believed to give life and drive out disease. One of the most famous and splendid of India's early temples is the temple of Surya at Konarak.

FOR DISCUSSION

1 Why do you think the caste system developed in India? Why were the warrior caste originally the top caste? Why do you think the priestly brahmin caste took over?

2 Many primitive religions worshipped the forces of nature as gods. Can you think of reasons why this should be so?

Part of a manuscript of the Rig Veda

2 Revealed Scriptures

Hindu literature consists of four collections of hymns known as the *Vedas* (Veda = knowledge), together with other material called Brahmanas, Aranyakas and Upanishads. These ancient revealed scriptures, originally written in Sanskrit, are called *sruti* (that which is heard) because it was believed that the *rishis* (holy men) who originally composed them had heard them directly from the gods.

The brahmins had memorised a great body of hymns to the gods, which they chanted as part of the ritual of worship. These hymns were collected during the period 1500 – 1000 B.C.E., but were not written down until many centuries later. They told of the deeds of the gods and the conquest of India.

The four collections of Vedas are:

1 *The Rig Veda.* This consists of over one thousand hymns, composed between 1500 and 1000 B.C.E., in praise of the many gods of the Aryan Indians.

2 *The Sama Veda.* This is not so much a separate book as an arrangement of certain verses of the Rig Veda for use in worship.

3 *The Yajur Veda.* This document is later than the Rig Veda, and contains instructions for the rituals of sacrifice to be carried out by the brahmins.

10

4   *The Arthava Veda.* This is a collection of magical spells and charms to control the weather, defeat one's enemies, or bring good luck.

These four Vedas are together known as the *Samhitas*.

The *Brahmanas* (priestly writings) are commentaries on the Samhitas. The *Aranyakas* (forest stories) grew out of the complexities of early Hinduism. The religious ritual which had developed under the influence of the brahmins had become very complicated, and many people wanted to find a simpler, purer form of religion. They went off alone into the forests to pray and meditate, and their writings were collected together to form the Aranyakas. Other religious people sat down with a *guru* (teacher) and discussed religious matters. These discussions were written down and formed the *Upanishads*, meaning "to sit down near".

Modern gurus still sit and teach their pupils. Here a guru is talking to a group on a rooftop in India

FOR DISCUSSION

1   The brahmins developed a complex ritual of sacrifice to the gods in their sacred writings. Do you know of other religions where sacrifice was important?

2   Why do you think some people took to the forests in search of an alternative form of religion? Can you think of any present-day forms of religion which involve solitude and isolation from the world?

Savitar, the sun god, being drawn by a seven-headed horse

3   The Rig Veda

The Rig Veda is a collection of hymns to the gods of the Aryan Indians. Most of those gods were personifications of the forces of nature. The following verse is known as the *Gayatri Mantra* (gaya = prayer, tri = three, mantra = verse). It is repeated three times daily by many Hindus in their worship.

"We meditate upon the adorable radiance of the resplendent life-giver, Savitar: may he stir up our thoughts."

(Rig Veda, III. 62:10)

12

The Rig Veda was intended for use in the worship of the gods, which was based on sacrifice. An essential element in sacrifice is fire, which burns away the offerings and so carries them up to the gods. The first hymn of the Rig Veda is devoted to Agni, the god of fire. (Note the similarity to the Latin word *ignis*, fire, root of the English word ignite, to set on fire.)

A sculpture of Agni

The Aryan sky god, Varuna, came to be looked upon as the upholder of order in the universe — not just as the governor of the regular cycle of days and seasons, but also of the moral law governing right behaviour. One of the hymns to Varuna has the following verse :

"If we have sinned against those who love us, or have wronged a brother, friend or comrade, a neighbour, or even a stranger, oh Varuna, take away our sin."   (Rig Veda, V. 85:7)

In Hindu worship today, the first action is the kindling of the sacred fire. Liquid butter (called *ghee*) is poured on the fire as the priest chants passages from the Vedas.

FOR DISCUSSION

1 The Gayatri Mantra is still used by countless Hindus as part of their daily worship. What is the difference between sun-worship and the reciting of this mantra?

2 Can you think of any other rituals or festivals in which fire is an important element? Why was fire so vital to primitive people?

3 The passage quoted from the hymn to Varuna is about seeking forgiveness. Do you know of any similar prayers or passages of scripture in other religions? Why do you think concern for forgiveness is such a universal theme?

Part of a manuscript of the Chandogya Upanishad

4 The Upanishads

There were many Upanishads written in Sanskrit between the seventh and second centuries B.C.E., but only about ten of them are regarded as important enough to be studied today. Most of them are written as dialogues between the guru and the follower, and although no clear-cut philosophy emerges from these dialogues, several important themes recur.

The first and most important theme of the Upanishads is the concept of *Brahman*, the spirit underlying the universe:

"Let us know that highest great lord of lords, the highest god among gods, the master of masters, the highest above, as god, the lord of the world, the adorable.

He is the one God, hidden in all beings, all-pervading, the self within all beings, watching over all works, dwelling in all beings, the witness, the perceiver, the only one, indefinable."

(Svetasvatara Upanishad, VI, 7, 11)

The second theme of the Upanishads is the quest of the soul to be at one with Brahman. The concept of *moksha*, freedom from all earthly bonds, first appears in the Upanishads, and the idea is taken up and developed in the Bhagavad Gita. The great prayer of the

14

Upanishads is to realise one's destiny as part of the supreme reality:

"From the unreal lead me to the real,
From darkness lead me to light,
From death lead me to immortality."
(Brihadaranyaka Upanishad, I. 3:28)

A third theme in the Upanishads is that of *karma-samsara*. Karma means deeds or actions, and samsara refers to a cycle of rebirth. Traditional Indian thought holds that the quality of a person's deeds will be directly linked to his or her next birth:

"Those whose conduct here has been good will quickly attain a good birth, as a brahmin, kshatriya or vaishya (merchant). But those whose conduct here has been evil will quickly attain an evil birth, the birth of a dog, the birth of a hog, or the birth of an out-caste." (Chandogya Upanishad)

FOR DISCUSSION

1   Hinduism, especially early Hinduism, is often called polytheistic, because of the many gods worshipped. Yet in the Upanishads, the notion of one God —

A statue of Brahman at Khajuraho, India

Brahman — emerges. How can both expressions of Hinduism be true? Can you think of parallels in other religions?

2   What do you think of the Hindu belief in karma-samsara? Do you know any accounts of experiences which would support belief in a cycle of rebirth?

It is easy to confuse three words which have the same root:
Brahman is the word used for Absolute Reality; the nearest equivalent word in English is God.
Brahma is the creator, one of the forms of Brahman. Brahma, Siva and Vishnu are the three main forms of Brahman.
A *brahmin* is a human being, a member of the priestly caste.

5 The Ramayana

In Hinduism, the traditional scriptures, called *smriti* (remembered), consist of two long poems, the *Ramayana* and the *Mahabharata*, and a collection of tales about the gods called the *Puranas*.

The Ramayana is an epic — a long, narrative poem — which tells the story of the good Prince Rama and his virtuous wife Sita. Rama should have succeeded to his father's throne, but is cheated of his inheritance and goes into exile with Sita and his brother Lakshmana. The demon Ravana carries Sita off to his island kingdom of Sri Lanka, and Rama and Lakshmana search for her in vain.

Hanuman, the monkey god, and his army of monkeys help Rama to cross the sea to Sri Lanka, where Rama kills Ravana with an arrow. Rama and Sita finally return in triumph to claim the kingdom.

The Ramayana is a story of courage against adversity, of kingly heroism and womanly virtue. It is also the classic story of the victory of good over evil, which perhaps explains why it is still so popular. It is acted, danced, and retold in many different forms, and Rama's defeat of Ravana is the basis of the festival of Dussehra. In this festival, however, it is the goddess Durga, wife of the god Siva, who helps Rama to rescue Sita.

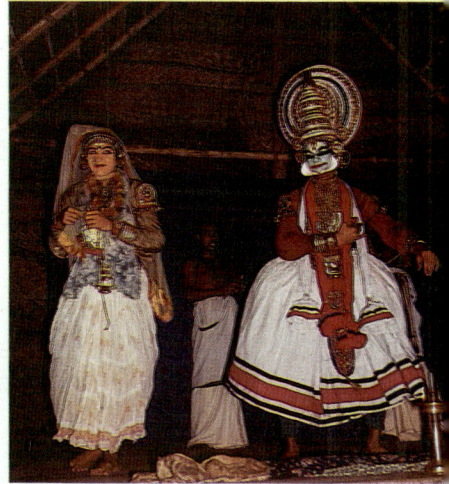

Kathikali dancers performing the Ramayana

FOR DISCUSSION

1 What is the difference between sruti and smriti?

2 How many epic tales do you know of? Which is your favourite? In what forms are epic tales handed on today? What accounts for their popularity?

3 There are many stories, in all religious traditions, of the conflict between good and evil. Why do you think this is? What fundamental beliefs do you think the composers of the Ramayana were trying to convey? Do these beliefs clash in any way with the other fundamental beliefs of Hinduism?

◀ *Rama and Sita with Hanuman*

A page opening of the Bhagavad Gita

6   The Mahabharata

The Mahabharata is the story of a long struggle for power between rival families of the Bharata tribe, one of the main tribes of the original Aryan invaders. It is the world's longest poem, consisting of 100 000 verses arranged in eighteen books, and written in Sanskrit.

In the story, the true heirs to the throne are the five sons of Pandu, but they are denied their birthright by their cousins. The two sides eventually meet in a great battle on the plain north of Delhi.

The Mahabharata is older than the Ramayana, having been composed originally in the ninth century B.C.E., although it was developed and added to considerably over the following centuries. It may well have been inspired by a real battle which took place at Kurukshetra (near to where Delhi now stands) about 900 B.C.E.

One book of the Mahabharata, added about 200 B.C.E., has become the most important and influential of all Hindu scriptures: the *Bhagavad Gita*. In this book, Arjuna, one of the five sons of Pandu, is in his chariot as the armies are preparing for battle, when he is suddenly overcome by the horror of fighting against his cousins.

18

Arjuna and Krishna on the battlefield

He orders his charioteer to retreat from the battle, but instead of obeying, the charioteer reminds Arjuna of his duties as a warrior. His body may die, but the body is merely clothing for the soul:

"As a man lays aside worn-out garments and puts on new clothes, so the soul puts away the body that has died and enters a new body." (Bhagavad Gita, II. 22)

Gradually, Arjuna comes to realise that his charioteer is no mere mortal, but an *avatar* (a god in human form) of Krishna. The Bhagavad Gita contains, in the form of dialogue between Krishna and Arjuna, all the main elements of Hindu devotion, and it is a powerful statement of the way to oneness with Brahman through *dharma* (the duties of one's caste):

"Neither for the sake of pleasure, nor for fear or greed, not even to save your own life should you give up dharma. Dharma lasts for ever; pleasure and pain are temporary."

FOR DISCUSSION

1   Do you think that the message of the Bhagavad Gita, to accept the duties of one's caste, is still appropriate today? The caste system was clearly important to social order when the Aryans conquered India; do you know how far the social structure of India has changed today? Is change a good thing, do you think?

2   The charioteer was an avatar of Krishna. Can you think of other religions in which God or gods appear on earth? What features do these accounts have in common? How far should they be believed? Does it matter if the stories are not literally true?

19

The fish, an avatar of Vishnu, saving Manu from the flood

7 The Laws of Manu

There are several ways in Hinduism to perform one's moral duty and achieve oneness with God. These ways are called *yogas*, from the Sanskrit word for union.

The first yoga is called *bhakti* (devotion), and this is given its fullest statement in the Bhagavad Gita. Arjuna devotes himself to Krishna, and sees in Krishna all the many forms of God:

"Ah my God, I see all gods in you,
All the multitudes of created beings,
Lord Brahman seated upon the lotus-throne,
All the wise men and the heavenly serpent."

(Bhagavad Gita, XI. 15)

It is interesting to see this age-old way of devotion revived in the Hare Krishna movement today.

The second yoga is called *karma marga* — the way of works. Karma means good deeds, as outlined in the Upanishads, but it refers also to obedience to religious ritual. The rules for religious ritual are given in precise detail in the *Laws of Manu*, which were written about the same time as the Bhagavad Gita. Manu is said to have been one of the ancient rishis to whom the Vedas were revealed.

The Laws of Manu lay down specific duties for the four castes:

"In order to preserve his world, God gave separate duties to the classes which emerged from his mouth, his arms, his thighs and his feet.

The brahmins are to teach, to study, and to perform sacrifices.

The kshatriya should protect people, distribute wealth, study and sacrifice, and lead a life of self-denial.

A vaishya should tend cattle, and look after all matters of trade, commerce and agriculture, as well as study and sacrifice.

The Lord has decreed only one occupation for a *shudra* (labouring class), that of serving the other three classes."

(Laws of Manu, I. 87-98)

There are many stories of Manu in the Puranas, including the story of Manu and the fish, in which a great fish saves Manu from a flood. This is very like the story of Noah's Ark in the Jewish and Christian religions.

FOR DISCUSSION

1   Why do you think many Western people, including pop stars, have turned to Hinduism and the East for inspiration?

2   There are codes of law governing human behaviour in most religions. Why do you think this is?

The four-headed Brahma (left), Vishnu (centre) and Siva (right) seated on lotus flowers

8 The Puranas

There are many tales of the gods of the Vedas which do not come from the Vedas themselves, but from collections of stories written about a thousand years ago. These are called *Puranas*; the word purana means "ancient".

In the Puranas, the great underlying principle of the Universe, Brahman, is seen in three main forms: Brahma, the Creator; Vishnu, the Preserver; and Siva (pronounced Shiva) the Destroyer.

Brahma, the Creator, is a shadowy figure, not much worshipped in Hinduism. One Puranic story tells how the goddess Sarasvati was trying to hide from him because he wanted to make love to her. Brahma grew four heads to look for her. To punish him, the gods decided he should no longer be worshipped.

The second way in which Brahman is worshipped is as Vishnu, the Preserver. Vishnu is said to have appeared in nine different forms. Not all sources agree, but generally these forms include: the fish which saved Manu from the flood; a tortoise which helped to find valuable articles lost in the flood; the boar which saved the earth from a demon; a man-lion; a goose; and a dwarf. Vishnu also became Rama, the hero of the Ramayana, and Krishna, the charioteer of Arjuna in the Bhagavad Gita. There are many stories of Krishna in the Puranas. In some of them he appears as a handsome, blue-skinned youth who plays a flute and flirts with the Gopis, beautiful maidens who herd cattle on the banks of the Ganges. The ninth avatar of Vishnu is said to have been the Buddha.

Siva dancing in a circle of flame

Siva, the Destroyer, is the third major form of Brahman. He is seen here in a flaming circle which stands for the universe. He is crushing a dwarf-demon underfoot. His flowing hair supports the river Ganges, which he caught when it fell from heaven. His upper right arm holds a flame, symbol of destruction. Siva is married to Parvati, daughter of the Himalayan mountains, who is also the goddess Durga or Kali, mother of the universe.

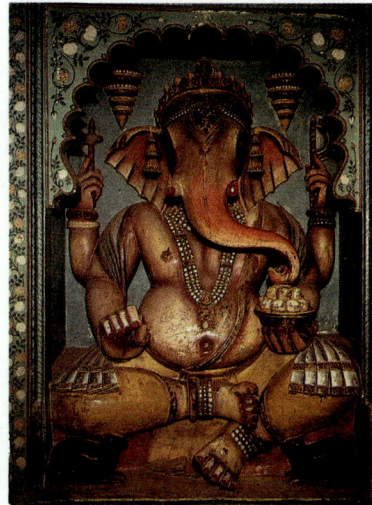

Ganesha, the god of wisdom

Their children are Kartikkeya, the god of war, and Ganesha, the elephant-headed god of wisdom, the one who blesses all new things.

FOR DISCUSSION

1 It is said that there is only one temple to Brahma in the whole of India. Why do you think Brahma is not as popular as, say, Ganesha, the elephant-headed god?

2 Vishnu is a very popular god in Hinduism. Which of his avatars would you say is the most popular? Which appeals to you most?

23

A carving of an early Jain "ford-finder" in a cave temple, India

9 Mahavira

Hinduism is such an ancient religion that it is not possible to point to any historical person or persons who founded it. By the seventh century B.C.E., however, it is possible to identify key religious figures, not only in Hinduism but in many religions around the world. This is so influential a period in the development of religious thinking that it has been called the "Axis Time". The first great philosophers of Ancient Greece, the prophets of Israel, and the sages Lao-Tzu and Confucius in China, all emerged around this time. In India, there were many teachers and religious leaders who made their mark, but none more so than Mahavira, founder of Jainism, and Gautama, founder of Buddhism. Both began in the Hindu tradition, and both were later to be regarded as heretics because they did not acknowledge the authority of the Vedas, and they refused to accept the caste system.

24

According to Jain traditions, there was a long line of "ford-finders" who discovered a way across the stream of human misery to the distant shores of salvation. The earliest of these are lost in the mists of prehistory, but the twenty-third ford-finder, Parshva, can be positively identified as a historical figure; he lived about 800 B.C.E.

However, the founder of Jainism as a separate sect was Mahavira (Great Hero). His real name was Nataputta, and he was born about 540 B.C.E. in Magadha (present-day Bihar). Nataputta was brought up as a noble, but after the death of his parents he joined a band of monks, followers of Parshva. In complete contrast to his earlier life of luxury, Nataputta now began to live as an ascetic, that is, one who spurns all comforts. He went homeless, unclothed, and often without food. After twelve years, he

A statue of Parshva

finally achieved *nirvana*, a state free from desire and suffering (from the Sanskrit word meaning "be extinguished"). From then on he was known as Mahavira.

FOR DISCUSSION

1   The Axis Time was a great flowering of human thought across the world. Why do you think this happened? Do you know of any other periods in human history when mankind has taken great leaps forward, in different countries and parts of the world?

2   For Mahavira, the "ford" to freedom and salvation was the way of extreme asceticism — poverty, hardship and suffering. Can you think of any other religious leaders who gave up everything in the pursuit of truth? Why is it that religious teachers often regard material possessions as an obstacle to spiritual growth?

A statue of Mahavira

10 Jainism

After he had achieved nirvana, Mahavira set out on a thirty-year period of teaching in which he sought to share his discovery that the "ford" to enlightenment was the path of extreme hardship and suffering — the "Jain path".

Jain teaching is contained in a number of books called *Agamas* (rules). One of the fundamental rules of Jainism is that its followers should avoid all human comforts:

"If when he is out begging he gets no food, he shouldn't worry; he should say, 'I have nothing today, I may get food tomorrow'.

"When a disciple, even though used to hardship, lies on the

rough grass, his body will feel the pain; in the full heat of the sun, the pain will be intense. Still he should wear no clothes."

(from the Sutrakritanga)

The second fundamental rule of Jainism is the principle of *ahimsa*, the avoiding of injury to all living things.

"He should cease to injure living beings, whether they move or not, in the air, on the ground, or below the ground."

(from the Sutrakritanga)

Mahavira used to carry a small broom with him, to brush insects from his path; today, his followers will wear a piece of cheesecloth over the mouth, to avoid breathing in any living creatures.

This doctrine of non-injury to living things leads Jains to reject the existence of God. If God made the world out of love for living beings, Jains argue, how can it be that living creatures suffer and die?

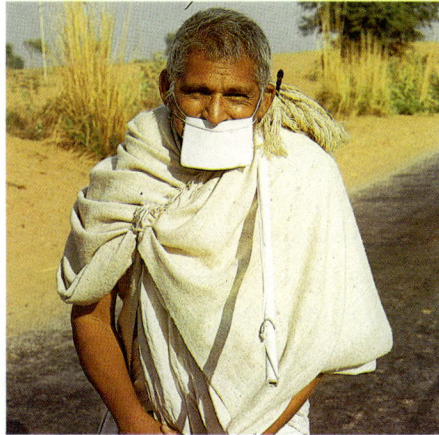

A Jain monk wearing a mouth mask

"Some foolish people say that God made the world.
This is nonsense, and should be rejected.
If God made the world, where was he before the Creation? . . .
If God made the world out of love for living things,
Why did he not make life blissful and free from suffering?"

(from the Gaina Sutra)

The Jain ideal is to attain the perfect soul, achieved through many lives of discipline and self-denial.

FOR DISCUSSION

1   Few people carry the doctrine of ahimsa (non-violence) as far as the Jains. Do you think the world would be a better place if everyone followed this belief? How would it affect your life if you tried to avoid doing injury to all living things?

2   If you believe in God, how would you counter the arguments of a Jain that God does not exist?

27

Things to do — Hinduism

1   The Aryan invaders of India believed in gods who were personifications of the forces of nature: Indra, the storm-god; Varuna, the sky-god; Savitar, the sun-god; and many others. Each of these gods was seen as having an influence over human beings. Indra was the god of war, Varuna the god of law and order, and Savitar the bringer of life and health. Write a short story about an incident in the life of an Aryan family, bringing in these gods. Perhaps you could start with a battle in which one of the sons is wounded.

2   There are four sorts of revealed scriptures in Hinduism — Vedas, Brahmanas, Aranyakas, Upanishads. Divide the class into four groups, each group taking one of these types of scripture. Think of a way of illustrating your scripture by means of a short mime or a tableau (like a "still" picture from a film). Remember, the Vedas were hymns composed by holy men; the Brahmanas were written by priests, and were rules for religious rituals; the Aranyakas were forest tales, written by holy men who went off alone into the forest; and the Upanishads were the teachings of the gurus, written down by their disciples.

3   In your own words, write a song of praise to the Sun God, Savitar.

4   The Upanishads contain the important themes of Brahman (absolute reality), moksha (freedom from earthly bonds and oneness with Brahman), and karma-samsara (deeds or actions, and the cycle of rebirth). Imagine the life of one individual soul through a series of rebirths, finally achieving moksha. Each person in the class should then choose one incident from this life and draw a picture of it. Then connect up all the pictures to make a frieze round the room, finishing with the achievement of being one with Brahman. (This is quite difficult to put into words or pictures; have a class discussion first to see how you might best depict it.)

5   Write out a scene from the Ramayana, or make up an episode from an epic tale of your own. You could work on this in a small group of four or five, and then act it out to the rest of the class. If each group's episode leads on to the next group's, you could build this up into a short play which might be suitable for an assembly.

The Trimurti — a three-headed statue of Siva in the Elephanta Caves, Maharashtra

6   The Laws of Manu give the rules for the yoga (way) called karma marga — the way of good deeds, or duty. It sets out the duties of the four castes — the priests, the warriors, the merchants, and the labourers. Draw a picture of each of these castes, and list their duties according to the Laws of Manu.

7   Draw a picture of Siva dancing in a flaming circle, and explain the symbolism of all the details in your drawing.

8   Draw an outline map of the world, and mark on it the names of the great thinkers who emerged during the Axis Time (seventh – sixth centuries B.C.E.). Put their names on the map in their country of origin.

9   Divide into groups of three. In each group, one person plays the part of a Hindu, who believes in Brahman and the three main forms in which Brahman is experienced (Brahma the creator, Vishnu the preserver and Siva the destroyer), one plays the part of a Jain, who doesn't believe in God at all, and the third person takes the role of an agnostic — that is, someone who isn't sure what to believe. Act out a discussion in which the Hindu and the

Jain try to persuade the agnostic that what they believe is right. The Hindu and the Jain are allowed to argue with each other, and the agnostic should not just sit quietly, but should join in the debate by asking questions.

10 Write an essay summarising the arguments in the debate in Question 9, and giving your own conclusions.

Buddhism

Like Jainism, Buddhism grew out of Hinduism; like Jainism, it owes its origin to a historical figure from the Axis Time. Unlike Jainism, however, Buddhism outgrew its parent; the Jains have remained a small sect of less than two million followers, all within India, whereas Buddhism has over 400 million adherents all over the world. This section examines the early texts of Buddhism, the life of the founder, Gautama Buddha, later stories about the Buddha, and some examples of his teaching.

An example of early Buddhist art in the crypt of the Temple of the Tooth, Sri Lanka

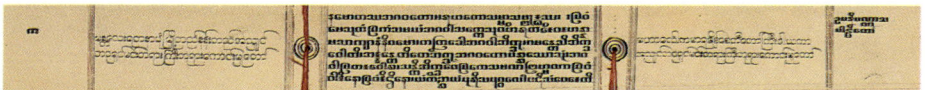

Part of the Sutta Pitaka from the Pali Canon. It is written on palm leaf. The pieces of palm leaf are then threaded on top of each other (the red strips are the threads) and are topped with boards to keep them flat. This version is written in ink and was commissioned by King Mindon, the founder of Mandalay in Burma. The centre section is the text of the Sutta Pitaka. Other versions of the Pali Canon are produced by engraving the palm leaf with a metal stylus and then rubbing charcoal into the impressions.

11   Schools of Buddhism

There is plenty of evidence that Buddhism owes its origins to a historical figure, Gautama, who lived in the Axis Time. Unfortunately, however, the founder of Buddhism left no writings of his own. Gautama Buddha died in 483 B.C.E., and for nearly five hundred years his teachings were preserved by word of mouth. Groups of Buddhist monks would chant the teachings together — thought to be a very accurate way of preserving them.

There were soon many different "schools" of Buddhism, as the teaching spread across India and into neighbouring countries. By the third century B.C.E., there were twelve schools of Buddhism in countries such as Sri Lanka, Burma and Thailand which recited the scriptures in the Pali language. This group is known as *Theravada* Buddhism (Theravada = teaching of the elders). To the north-west of India and in countries such as China, Japan and Vietnam, however, Buddhism was beginning to change. In these countries, six schools of Buddhism developed which celebrated the Buddha's teaching in the Sanskrit language. These schools were more open to ordinary people than the Theravada schools, and their way became known as *Mahayana* Buddhism (Maha = great, yana = way of salvation).

The Buddhist scriptures were not written down until the first century B.C.E., although fragments of Buddhist texts have been found on stone monuments put up by the Emperor Asoka in about 250 B.C.E. The scriptures of the Theravada Buddhists are known as the Pali Canon, and these survive today.

FOR DISCUSSION

1   Why do you think the teachings of the Buddha were not written down for so long? How accurately do you think the Buddha's teachings were preserved during this time? Do you know of other examples of religious teachings handed down by word of mouth?

2   By about the thirteenth century C.E., Buddhism was firmly established in many Eastern countries, but had virtually disappeared from India. Can you think of any reasons for this?

A statue of a seated Buddha at a temple in Sri Lanka

12   The Tipitaka

The Pali Canon, the scriptures of Theravada Buddhism, is divided into three parts, the *Tipitaka* (three baskets). These are:

The *Vinaya Pitaka*: rules for Buddhist monks.

The *Sutta Pitaka*: teachings of the Buddha.

The *Abhidhamma Pitaka*: commentary on the teachings.

Of the three, the oldest and probably the most important for an understanding of Buddhism is the Sutta Pitaka. This consists mainly of sermons by the Buddha, and is arranged in five collections of essays. The last section, which has two parts, contains the heart of Buddhist teaching. Part one is the *Dhammapada*, or "Path of Virtue". The Dhammapada has 423 verses, which most Buddhists can recite from memory. It contains the Buddha's teaching of the Four Noble Truths, and the Noble Eightfold Path.

The oldest surviving complete Pali text is a copy of the Dhammapada, written on birch bark and dating back to the second

Buddhist monks today, with a boy who is about to become a monk

century C.E. The Buddha was, of course, familiar with the Hindu concepts of karma and samsara (moral deeds and rebirth), and in the Dhammapada he explains these ideas:

> "As rust upon iron eats into itself, so do their own deeds bring evil-doers to a sorry end."   (Dhammapada, 240)

Part two of the last section of the Sutta Pitaka contains stories of previous lives of the Buddha, called the *Jataka* stories. One of these describes the birth of the Buddha, let down from the clouds in a golden net held by four gods, who are chanting: "Great Buddha, great above all other." According to the story, the baby immediately stood up, took seven steps, and roared like a lion, saying, "I am Buddha, the Mighty One."

FOR DISCUSSION

1   Why do you think the three parts of the Pali Canon are called the Tipitaka (three baskets)?

2   The communities of monks who were followers of the Buddha left their families and went to live in monasteries. Why do you think a code of rules was needed?

3   The Jataka stories are much later than the Dhammapada, and were probably written by Buddhist monks and nuns. Many stories about great religious leaders grow up after their death. Why do you think this is? Can you think of examples from other religions? What is more important — whether such stories are literally true, or whether they convey truths about the nature and purpose of mankind?

A statue of the Buddha in Rangoon, seated beneath a tree grown from a seed brought from his birthplace

13   Gautama Buddha

Siddhartha Gautama was born in 563 B.C.E., the son of a local ruler in the country now called Nepal, north of India. He was brought up in luxury and was protected by his father from all the harsh realities of life. At the age of sixteen he married the beautiful Yashodara.

However, the easy life left Siddhartha Gautama unsatisfied. The traditional story tells how the young prince left the palace in the company of a servant, and saw for the first time a man racked with disease, then a very old man on the point of death, and finally a corpse being taken away to be cremated. He was deeply disturbed by these encounters with suffering and death, and made up his mind to try and find an answer to the problem of suffering.

Leaving his home, Gautama spent some time sitting at the feet of leading Hindu gurus. Dissatisfied with their answers, he then spent six years as an ascetic, giving up all human comforts. During this time, Gautama punished his body until he was on the point of death, but he was still no nearer to solving the problem of suffering. He made up his mind to sit cross-legged under a pipal (fig) tree until he found an answer.

For many days, Gautama sat alone, deep in meditation. Tradition says he was attacked by an evil demon, Mara, whose attacks ranged from whirlwind and storm to the more subtle temptations of Mara's three daughters, Desire, Pleasure and Passion. Eventually Mara gave up, and after forty-nine days Gautama knew the answer to human misery and what must be done to overcome it. He had become *Buddha*, the Enlightened One, and the tree under which he sat became known as the *Bo-Tree* — the tree of knowledge.

FOR DISCUSSION

1   Why do you think Siddhartha's father tried to keep him from contact with human suffering and death? In many ways, we in the western world today try to avoid thinking about death. Do you think we ought to face up to reality? Do you ever think about death and the purpose of life?

2   What sort of temptations did Siddhartha face? Can you think of examples from other religions where people spent time alone struggling against temptation?

3   The fundamental problem which Siddhartha Gautama confronted is one which all great religions and philosophies tackle in different ways: the problem of suffering and death. It is particularly difficult for those religions which teach belief in God. How can a loving God allow his creatures to suffer? What are your thoughts on this?

The Mahabodhi Temple at Bodh Gaya, built on the place where the Buddha achieved enlightenment

14 The Jataka Stories

After he had achieved enlightenment, the Buddha stayed on earth a further forty-five years teaching his new way of salvation, the "Middle Way". He died in 483 B.C.E. at the age of eighty, and before long, legends about him began to grow and develop. Eventually, he came to be seen as one of a long line of Buddhas, who had been born again and again until all the perfect qualities of the Buddha developed. These accounts of previous lives of the Buddha were collected together in the Jataka stories, many of which tell how the Buddha often risked his life to save others. In the following story, he puts himself in grave danger to save a friend:

Once upon a time there were three friends — an antelope, who lived in a forest near a lake; a woodpecker; and a terrapin, who lived in the mud at the bottom of the lake. One night, when he came down to the lake to drink, the antelope was caught in a leather trap set by a hunter. The woodpecker and the terrapin heard his cries and came to see what was the matter.

They tried everything they could think of to open the trap, but it was too strong for them. Eventually, the woodpecker had an idea.

'See if you can chew through these straps with your strong teeth, friend terrapin,' he said. 'I will try to stop the hunter from coming.'

The terrapin set to work on the leather straps, while the woodpecker flew off to the hunter's house. When he saw the hunter coming out, the woodpecker dived at his face, screeching loudly. The hunter hastily ducked back into his house. The woodpecker managed to delay the hunter in this way for some time, and then flew back to the lakeside to warn his friends.

The terrapin had been chewing away at the leather trap all night, and he was exhausted. The antelope managed to break free just as the hunter, knife in hand, was creeping up to the trap.

The hunter found the trap empty, with the exhausted terrapin lying beside it. Disappointed, he decided to take the terrapin instead, and tossed it into his bag. The antelope, seeing what had happened, decided that he must now try to save his friend. He came out of the trees so that the hunter could see him. As he had hoped, the hunter threw down his bag and chased after him. The antelope led the hunter deeper and deeper into the forest, then doubled back quickly and freed the terrapin.

FOR DISCUSSION

1   In the story of the three friends, which do you think was the previous incarnation of the Buddha? Can you think of any other fables or folk tales like this one?

2   Why do you think the Jataka stories developed? Which particular Hindu and Buddhist belief is essential to such stories?

The moonstone and eight steps at the Vata Daga Temple, Polonnaruva, Sri Lanka

15   The Teaching of the Buddha

After he had achieved Enlightenment, the Buddha began to teach others what he had discovered. His first sermon was in the Deer Park at Benares in northern India. This sermon, said to be preserved in the Dhammapada (Path of Virtue), contains the main elements of the Buddha's new Way of Salvation, the "Middle Way", which avoided the two extremes of asceticism (giving everything up) and sensuality (wanting the pleasures of life).

The Middle Way consists of the *Four Noble Truths*:

1 *All life is suffering*. Life is never as we would wish it to be. All pleasures are short-lived, and all experience is pain, suffering and, eventually, death.

2 *Suffering is caused by desire*. This means the selfish desires and cravings of mankind, which have brought about human misery.

3 *Suffering can be ended if desire is overcome*. The state which is achieved when all desire and suffering have ceased is called *nirvana*. This is the goal of Buddhism.

4 *There is a way to overcome desire*. This is the Buddha's way of wisdom, morality and meditation.

This "way" outlined by the Buddha was later described in more detail as the *Noble Eightfold Path*:

1 Right understanding ⎫
2 Right thought   ⎬ Wisdom

3 Right speech   ⎫
4 Right action   ⎬ Morality
5 Right livelihood ⎭

6 Right mental effort ⎫
7 Right mindfulness   ⎬ Meditation
8 Right concentration ⎭

The moonstone and eight steps at Polonnaruva are a kind of symbol of the teaching of Buddhism. The outer ring of the moonstone contains the flames of passion or desire which is at the heart of all suffering. The band of animals depicts the four perils of life: birth, disease, old age, and death. The eight steps symbolise the Noble Eightfold Path.

FOR DISCUSSION

1 What do you think of the Buddha's First Noble Truth? Does the idea that everything, even pleasurable experience, is overshadowed by the knowledge that it must come to an end, ring true to you? Can you think of any examples in the modern world of "background" thoughts and worries that prevent people from being happy and fulfilled?

2 The Second Noble Truth is difficult to express in English; the word "desire" is not really adequate. Think of other words or phrases to express what you think the Buddha really meant.

The Eastern Gateway of the Sanchi Stupa, on which events in the life of the Buddha are carved

Things to do — Buddhism

1   The teachings of the Buddha were preserved very accurately for five hundred years by word of mouth: groups of monks would chant the teachings together. Test this by learning one of the school rules by heart, and chanting it together as a class every morning for a week (or every time you have an R.E. lesson, for a month). Does it work? Why is it an accurate way of preserving teaching?

2   Unit 12 describes the scriptures of Theravada Buddhism, the Tipitaka. Draw a chart, showing the Vinaya Pitaka, the Sutta Pitaka, and the Abhidhamma Pitaka; and the two parts of the Sutta Pitaka, the Dhammapada and the Jataka stories.

3   Draw the traditional story of the life of the Buddha as a series of pictures, illustrating his early life as a prince, his marriage to Yashodara, his encounter with suffering, old age, and death, his time with Hindu gurus and ascetics, the period spent sitting under the pipal tree, the temptations of Mara and his three daughters, the Enlightenment, and his forty-five years as a teacher of the "Middle Way".

4   Write a short essay explaining the Buddhist concept of nirvana.

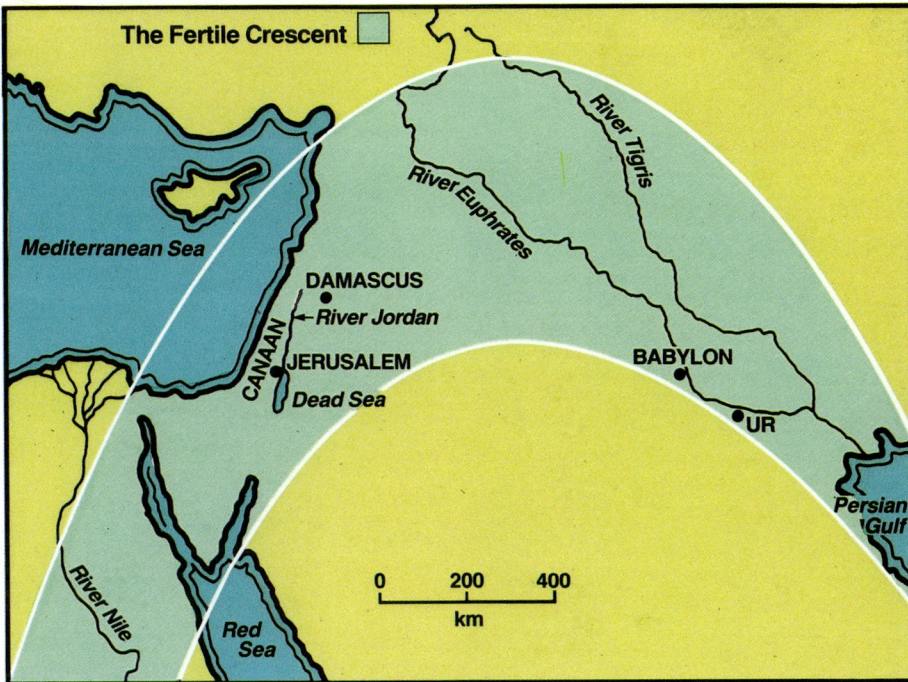

The Fertile Crescent map showing: The Fertile Crescent, Mediterranean Sea, River Tigris, River Euphrates, DAMASCUS, River Jordan, CANAAN, JERUSALEM, Dead Sea, BABYLON, UR, Persian Gulf, River Nile, Red Sea. Scale 0 200 400 km.

The Fertile Crescent

Judaism

Judaism is the religion of the Jewish people; but it is very difficult to say precisely who are the Jews. All the Jewish tribes in the early part of the Bible story are called Hebrews. About the year 2000 B.C.E., at a time when many tribes of people were nomads, a group of Hebrews led by Abraham left the town of Ur in Mesopotamia and followed the Fertile Crescent, eventually settling in Canaan, present-day Israel.

The grandson of Abraham, Jacob, was also called Israel, and the Hebrews came to be known as Israelites. Jacob had twelve sons, fathers of the twelve tribes of Israel. One of these sons was called Judah, and it is from Judah that the names Jew and Judaism come. Today, the name Jew may refer to someone who is Jewish by religion, or someone who is Jewish by descent but not necessarily religious, or someone who lives in the modern state of Israel.

This section looks at the historical development of the Jewish people and religion, and at the founders and prophets who inspired, wrote or feature in the sacred writings of the Jews.

43

Scrolls in the Ark of the Bennea Synagogue, Safed

16   The Tanak

The Jewish Bible is the same as the first part of the Christian Bible, the Old Testament. In Hebrew it is called the *Tanak*, and is made up of three parts:

Torah (Law or Teaching). This is the first five books, often called the Books of Moses. It is also known as the *Pentateuch*, which is Greek for "five books".

Nebiim (Prophets). This section is made up of the books about, and by, the various prophets of Israel.

Ketubim (Writings). This consists of eleven books of different kinds, such as Psalms, Proverbs and Chronicles.

The word Tanak is made up from the initial letters of these three words: *Torah, Nebiim and Ketubim.*

The scriptures which are used in Jewish worship today are written on scrolls, just as they were hundreds of years ago. The scrolls of the

Torah and the Book of Esther are still made from parchment. A scribe, who has made a careful study of the scriptures, writes out the text in Hebrew by hand. Hebrew is written from right to left, and originally it was written without vowels. The parchment is made from specially prepared calfskin, and the sheets of parchment are sewn together to make a scroll. This is fastened at each end to a wooden roller, known as "The Tree of Life". The wooden rollers are capped with silver crowns, and covered with a velvet cloth and a silver breastplate.

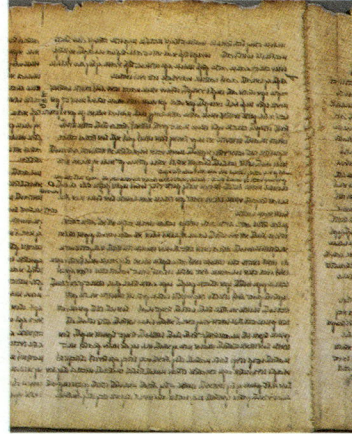

Part of the Dead Sea Scrolls

Few early scrolls of the Tanak exist, perhaps because the Jewish people have been persecuted over the centuries, and their books and possessions destroyed. The oldest complete scroll of a book of the Tanak is a scroll of Isaiah dating back to the second century B.C.E., found with many other scrolls in a cave near the Dead Sea in 1947.

The Tanak in its present form was put together in the sixth century B.C.E. by Ezra the Scribe and a group of people known as the Men of the Great Synagogue. The Israelites had been in exile in Persia, and when they began to return to their homeland in 538 B.C.E. they found their country in ruins. Ezra restored the Temple and the observance of the festivals, and his group arranged the sacred writings of the Jews to form the Tanak.

FOR DISCUSSION

1 Why do you think the Jewish sacred writings are treated by the Jews with such respect?
2 Why would you say that Ezra is known as "the father of modern Judaism"?
3 Jewish people have always read their sacred scripture in Hebrew, even though by the time of Jesus most Jews spoke Aramaic, and today Jews speak the language of the country in which they live. Why is it so important to Jews to preserve the original language?

Students, watched by their teacher, performing Hagbeh — the act of lifting the Torah to show it to the congregation

17   The Torah

The *Torah* contains the first five books of the Tanak, or Old Testament. Torah is often translated as "law", but a better translation is "teaching". To a Jew, this is the most important part of the Bible. It consists of five books: Genesis, Exodus, Leviticus, Numbers, Deuteronomy. These were for a long time thought to have been written by Moses, but many modern scholars, both Jewish and Christian, argue that in their present form they were written centuries later. Orthodox Jews still accept that Moses was the author of the Torah, and this, in effect, is the main difference between Orthodox and Progressive Judaism.

The Book of Genesis begins with two accounts of how the world was created: a formal version which speaks of God creating the world in seven "days", (Genesis 1, and 2, 1-4), and a much older story in Genesis 2, 5-25:

"One day the Lord God formed a man from the dust of the earth, and breathed life into him. The Lord called him *Adam* (man). Realising that Adam would have to have somewhere to live, the Lord planted a garden in the East and called it Eden."

After other ancient stories, the narrative comes to Noah, who was the first man with whom God made an agreement, or covenant. (The word "testament" also means agreement.) Because Noah has been righteous, God spares him and his family from a flood which destroys the rest of mankind.

The story now concentrates on Noah's descendants, traced through his son, Shem. This is the origin of the name Semites, another term for the Jewish and Arab peoples. We read of Abraham's journey to Canaan, and the birth of his son, Isaac. Abraham also had a covenant with God, as a token of which Isaac and all Abraham's male descendants were circumcised. This tradition continues today.

Isaac had two sons, Jacob and Esau, and Jacob's twelve sons are the ancestors of the twelve tribes of Israel. The story follows Jacob's favourite son, Joseph, and his adventures in Egypt. This explains how the Israelites found themselves as slaves in Egypt.

FOR DISCUSSION

1   Why do you think the two versions of the story of Creation, in Genesis 1 and 2, were put together? For a long time, people read these two stories as one continuous story, and it was not until the late nineteenth century that Biblical scholars teased the separate strands of Genesis apart. Some people still refuse to accept the scholars' findings, arguing that the Bible is the word of God, and it must all be true. What do you think?

2   The story of Noah's Ark is very similar to that of Manu and the Fish, in Hindu scripture. There are many similar flood stories in ancient literature. Why do you think this is a common theme?

3   At what point, in Genesis or later, would you say that myth and legend stop and history begins? (N.B. There is no agreed answer to this question!)

The Crossing of the Red Sea — "The Submersion of Pharaoh's Army" by Lucas Cranach

18 Exodus

The second book of the Torah, *Exodus* (going out), tells the story of Moses, an Israelite brought up as an Egyptian prince, whom God chose to lead the Israelites out of Egypt to the Promised Land:

> " 'I have seen the suffering of my people in Egypt,' God said. 'I am going to lead them out to a new land, which will be their own; a land where milk and honey are plentiful. You, Moses, will be their leader.' "
>
> (Exodus 3, 7-8) "

Moses was, by any reckoning, one of the great men of history. His name comes from the Hebrew word meaning "to pull out of water". There are many stories about his birth and the miraculous plagues by which he succeeded in persuading the Pharaoh (King) of Egypt to release the Israelites. The Israelites left Egypt by way of the Red Sea, or Sea of Reeds, the waters being held back by "a strong east wind"

(Exodus 14, 21). The song of triumph which follows is one of the oldest passages in the Bible:

"I will sing to the Lord, for he has triumphed gloriously;

The horse and his rider he has thrown into the sea." (Exodus 15, 1)

Moses led the Israelites to Mount Sinai, where a covenant was made between God and the people:

"'Speak to the sons of Jacob, the children of Israel,' the Lord said to Moses. 'They have seen how I led them out of Egypt, and brought them on eagles' wings to me. If they will listen to me and keep my commandments, I will make them my special people.'"

(Exodus 19, 3-5)

Moses engraved the Commandments of God on tablets of stone, and these laws of religion and behaviour became the basis of Jewish duty from then on:

"I am the Lord your God, who brought you out of slavery in Egypt.

You shall have no other gods but me.

You shall not worship idols or carved images of gods.

You must not misuse the name of the Lord your God, or He will punish you.

You must keep the Sabbath day holy. Work for six days, but do no work on the seventh day.

Respect your father and mother.

Do not commit murder.

Respect the marriage-bond.

Do not steal.

Do not lie or give false evidence against anyone.

Do not long for things which are not yours." (Exodus 20, 1-17)

FOR DISCUSSION

1   Jewish people still celebrate the Exodus from Egypt in the festival of *Pesach* (Passover). Why do you think this event is so important to them?

2   The Ten Commandments were first written at a time when people believed in many gods. How can you tell? Which of the Ten Commandments are still generally regarded as important by many non-Jewish people?

3   Can you see similarities between any of the Commandments and the Four Noble Truths of Buddhism in Unit 15?

A stained-glass window in Lincoln Cathedral, showing, left, the priests blowing their horns outside Jericho, and, right, piling the stones to mark the miraculous dry crossing of the Jordan

19 The Former Prophets — Joshua and Judges

The second part of the Tanak is the Nebiim, the Prophetic books. These Prophetic books are divided into:

The Former Prophets (Joshua, Judges, I and II Samuel, I and II Kings). These relate the history of Israel from the entry into the Promised Land to the fall of Jerusalem in 586 B.C.E.

The Latter Prophets (Isaiah, Jeremiah, Ezekiel, Hosea, Amos, and a number of shorter books of prophecy). These are covered in Unit 21.

The Books of Joshua and Judges describe, in contrasting and often contradictory ways, how the Israelites conquered Canaan. The Book of Joshua represents the settlement in Canaan as taking place swiftly and successfully during the lifetime of Joshua, the successor to Moses. The Book of Judges indicates that wars against various Canaanite tribes continued for centuries after Joshua's death.

Perhaps the early campaigns under Joshua met with initial success which had to be consolidated by later generations.

In order to enter Canaan, the Israelites had to cross the river Jordan. There have been various reports of the Jordan's banks collapsing and damming the river for a period; in 1927, the west bank collapsed near the Dead Sea and the Jordan was dammed for twenty-one hours. The first city that Joshua took was Jericho:

> " 'God has told me what to do,' Joshua told the Israelites. 'Follow my instructions, and Jericho is ours.'
>
> He put seven priests with trumpets in front of the Ark, a golden box containing the Commandments, then lined up all the fighting men from the tribes of Israel and ordered them to march round the city walls. This was repeated every day for six days. On the seventh day, the procession went round Jericho seven times. Then Joshua ordered the trumpets to sound, and the Israelites gave a tremendous shout and stormed the walls. The walls collapsed, and the city was theirs." (Joshua 6, 1-21)

From about 1200-1020 B.C.E., the Iron Age, the tribes of Israel were ruled over by Judges. One of these was a woman, a prophetess named Deborah. Judges 4 describes a famous battle in which Deborah's army, led by Barak, routed the army of the Canaanite king, Jabin, at Megiddo. Other well-known Israelite leaders during this period were Gideon, who defeated the Midianites with just three hundred men (Judges 7); and Samson, whose exploits against the Philistines are famous (Judges 13-16).

The Philistines, who gave their name to the land, Palestine, invaded Canaan from the west at about the same time as the Israelites invaded it from the east.

FOR DISCUSSION

1 The Bible describes Canaan as the land promised by God to the Israelites. The tribes living in Canaan at the time, and the Philistines in particular, obviously thought differently. What do you think? Can you see any present-day parallels?

2 What do you think happened at Jericho: an earthquake, psychological warfare, sound vibrations from the marching and the trumpets, or divine intervention?

David severing Goliath's head after hitting him with a stone from his sling, which is shown in the foreground — a ceiling panel in the Sistine Chapel, painted by Michelangelo

20   The Former Prophets — Samuel and Kings

These books cover about four hundred years of Jewish history, and focus on two great themes: Kingship and Prophecy, often with one in conflict with the other. It was Samuel, last and greatest of the Judges, who reluctantly decided that Israel should have a king. His first choice was the son of Kish, Saul, a tall, powerful man and a natural leader. Saul and his son Jonathan succeeded in uniting the tribes of Israel against the Philistines.

Saul's successor, David, first came to the fore as the shepherd-boy who succeeded in killing the giant Philistine Goliath with a sling and cut off Goliath's head with his victim's own sword. This illustrates the belief of the Israelites at that time, that the Lord was their god and that other tribes had other gods:

" 'You stand before me with weapons and armour,' cried David. 'But I stand here in the name of the Lord God of Israel, who will destroy you today. Then the whole world will know that there is a God in Israel!' "   (I Samuel 17, 45-46)

One of David's great achievements was to capture Jerusalem in about 990 B.C.E. The water-shaft which David and his men used to

52

take the city probably led from the Gihon spring. This was later enlarged by King Hezekiah, and it is possible to walk along the tunnel today.

Hezekiah's Tunnel, Jerusalem

David was succeeded by his son Solomon, who had a reputation for wisdom, and whose flair for administration and foreign policy brought Israel power and wealth never surpassed before or since. At the same time, his ambitious building programmes and forced-labour policy sowed the seeds of dissent which led, after his death, to the break-up of the kingdom. Jeroboam became king of the ten tribes to the north, and this became known as the kingdom of Israel; *Rehoboam* was king of the two tribes to the south, centred on Jerusalem, which became known as Judah.

One of Jeroboam's successors was Ahab, and the story of his clash with the prophet Elijah is typical. Ahab wanted Naboth's vineyard, but Naboth would not sell. Jezebel, Ahab's foreign wife, soon sorted the problem out; she had Naboth killed. Ahab was inspecting his new vineyard when he was suddenly confronted by the prophet Elijah.

" 'So you've found me out, have you?' Ahab said to Elijah.

'The Lord has found you out, Ahab,' said Elijah sternly. 'Because of what you have done, you and your royal house will be punished and destroyed. As for your wife, Jezebel, the dogs will lick up her blood here in the city of Jezreel, where they licked the blood of Naboth.' "

(I Kings 21, 20-21)

FOR DISCUSSION

1   Why do you think Samuel was reluctant to give Israel a king?

2   The idea of kingship became very influential in later Judaism. When the Jewish people were suffering and oppressed, they looked forward to the coming of a *Messiah* (Anointed One), a second David, who would defeat their enemies. Why do you think the memory of David is so strong?

3   Elijah, one of the earliest prophets, was quite prepared to speak out against the king, the Lord's anointed, if he thought the king was wrong. Do you think a prophet is someone who predicts the future or someone who speaks out, in the name of God?

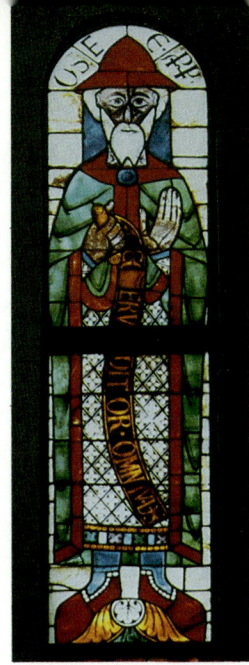

Two stained-glass windows, showing, left, the calling of Amos and, right, Hosea

21   The Latter Prophets

The eighth and seventh centuries B.C.E. saw the emergence of great prophets in Israel and Judah whose words were written down by their followers and preserved in the books we find in the Bible today — Amos, Hosea, Isaiah and Jeremiah (cf. the "Axis Time" in India and elsewhere, Unit 9). This was a time of wars and confusion, and the old gods of Canaan were still being worshipped at hilltop shrines all over the land. This practice was known as Baal-worship.

The prophets saw this as unfaithfulness to the Lord, and strongly condemned it. Hosea compared Israel to an unfaithful wife, and Amos criticised the Israelites for their evil ways:

"The crimes of Israel are unforgivable! They betray innocent people for a handful of silver, and steal the shoes from a beggar."

(Amos 2, 6)

Amos was a hill-farmer from Tekoa, near Jerusalem, but he felt that God had called him to prophesy in the northern kingdom of Israel:

"You fools! You wait for the Day of the Lord, but it will be a day of darkness, not light. It will be like a man running away from a lion and being caught by a bear, or going into his house for safety and being bitten by a snake."

(Amos 5, 18-19)

The "Day of the Lord" did indeed come for the kingdom of Israel in 721 B.C.E., when King Sargon II of Assyria destroyed the capital, Samaria, and deported the Israelite people.

The southern kingdom of Judah lasted rather longer, despite being assailed by enemies on all sides.

The remains of a Canaanite altar to Baal, near Megiddo

The prophet Isaiah urged King Ahaz to rely upon God:

"Do not be afraid of these two smouldering embers. The kings of Israel and Aram are burning with rage, but they will never take Judah. The Lord God will give you a sign: A young woman in this court is expecting a baby. The baby will be called Immanuel, 'God with us'. By the time the baby is weaned, the lands of Aram and Israel will be laid waste." (from Isaiah 7, 4-17)

Ahaz ignored Isaiah and made a pact with Assyria, despite the prophet's warning that:

"The Assyrian is the club God will use to beat you. The Lord will send him to plunder you and trample you underfoot like dust."
(Isaiah 10, 5-6)

Forty years later, in 688 B.C.E., the Assyrian King Sennacherib attacked Jerusalem, but Isaiah, by now an old man, prophesied that the city would survive:

"For the sake of his servant David, the Lord will deliver the city."
(Isaiah 37, 35)

FOR DISCUSSION

1 The prophets of the eighth and seventh centuries B.C.E. stressed the need for justice, fairness and honesty. How does this compare with the teaching of Mahavira and Gautama in India at about the same period?

2 Why were the prophets so offended by Baal-worship?

3 The prophets did warn of what might happen if the people ignored the word of God, but their prophecies were usually about what would happen in the immediate future. How have the prophecies of Isaiah been used by Christian writers?

Jeremiah — a ceiling panel in the Sistine Chapel, Rome, by Michelangelo

22 The Period of Exile

Jerusalem's survival, foretold by Isaiah, was short-lived. Assyria fell to the Babylonians in 612 B.C.E., and the prophet Nahum rejoiced over the destruction of the Assyrian city Nineveh:

"Then all who see it will turn away and say, 'Nineveh is laid waste; who will comfort her now?'" (Nahum 2, 7)

Before long, however, the Babylonians were at the gates of Jerusalem. The city fell in 586 B.C.E. and the Jews were transported to exile in Babylon. The prophet Jeremiah lived through this period, and foretold the destruction of Jerusalem:

"These are the words of the Lord God: 'Look at yourselves and the lives you lead, before you come into my house. You break my commandments, you lie, cheat and steal, you go after false gods, and then you come into my temple saying 'This is the temple of the Lord,' and imagine you will be safe here.

You gain nothing by putting your faith in these false beliefs. Because I gave you this temple, you think it will stand for all time, whatever you do. But you are wrong. Jerusalem will be laid waste and this temple will be destroyed." (Jeremiah 7)

Ezekiel calling the wind to breathe life into the bodies — a painting by Collantes

Ezekiel was one of the Jews carried off to exile in Babylon. Like Jeremiah, he also prophesied the fall of Jerusalem, but after the event his prophecies changed. God's punishment had come about, and Ezekiel had to look to the future. He had a dream in which God took him to a valley full of dried-out bones:

"'Human, do you see these bones?' God asked him. 'Could they ever live again?'

'Only you know that, Lord,' Ezekiel replied.

'Speak to the bones, human,' God commanded him. 'Tell them that the Lord will put muscle and flesh on them, and breathe into them, and they will come to life.'

Ezekiel, in his dream, did as God said, and as he spoke, flesh appeared on the bones and they became human bodies. Ezekiel ordered the wind to come and breathe into them; the bodies began to breathe, then came to life and stood up, a great host of people."   (Based on Ezekiel 37)

From then on, Ezekiel began to prophesy to the exiles that God would restore them to their own land.

FOR DISCUSSION

1   Why do you think the name Jeremiah is used today to signify someone who brings a message of unrelieved gloom? Is this a fair summary of the prophet Jeremiah's writings?

2   Why did the tone of Ezekiel's prophecies change after 586 B.C.E.?

3   What do you think Ezekiel's dream about the Valley of Dry Bones means?

57

Daniel in the Lions' Den — a painting by Rubens

23 The Writings — Daniel and Esther

The third section of the Tanak is the Ketubim, or Writings. This contains a wide variety of different kinds of literature: psalms, proverbs, wisdom literature, poetry, and history. Two of the books, Daniel and Esther, written in the second century B.C.E., are in fact historical novels, set in the time of exile four centuries before.

The Book of Daniel was set in Babylon at the time of King Nebuchadnezzar. Daniel was one of four Jewish noblemen taken to Babylon after the fall of Jerusalem. Because of his skill in interpreting dreams, Daniel was appointed regent over the whole province of Babylon, and his three companions, Shadrach, Meshach and Abed-nego, were also given important posts. But they refused to worship a statue erected by Nebuchadnezzar, and were brought before him:

" 'Is it true that you refuse to worship our god?' he asked.

'We can serve only one God,' Shadrach replied. 'If anyone can save us from the fire of the furnace, it is our God. But even if he cannot save us, we still will not worship your god.'

Nebuchadnezzar flew into a rage, and ordered his servants to heat up the furnace.

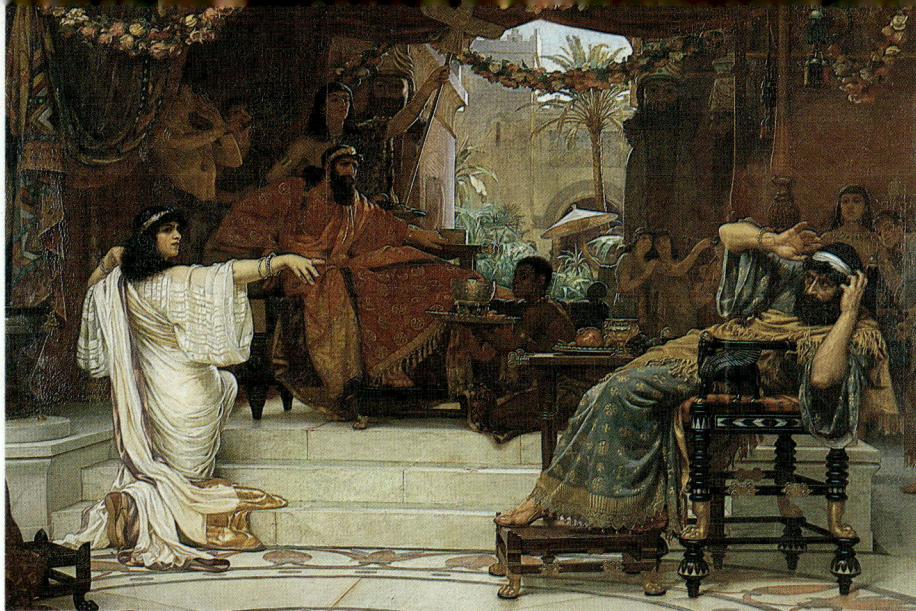

Esther denouncing Haman — a painting by Ernest Normand

'Now will you bow down to the god of Babylon?' he asked.

'Never!' the three replied.

'Throw them in!' the King roared." (Daniel 3, 14-23)

To everyone's amazement, the three survived the flames, and Nebuchadnezzar issued a decree that the Jews should be allowed to worship in their own way.

Another part of the story had a similar theme: Daniel was thrown into a lions' den because he worshipped a 'foreign' god, and he also survived.

The Book of Esther is the story of a Jewish girl, and it is set in Persia about 500 B.C.E. (The Persians defeated the Babylonians in 539 B.C.E.) It is interesting to note that the modern name for Persia, Iran, has the same origin as Aryan — the people who invaded India about 500 B.C.E. Esther became the wife of King Xerxes, and she and her uncle Mordecai managed to thwart an evil plot by Haman, the king's chief adviser, to kill the Jews. This story is celebrated today in the Jewish festival of *Purim*.

FOR DISCUSSION

1 Why do you think the writers of Daniel and Esther gave their books a historical setting?

2 Can you deduce, from the storylines of Daniel and Esther, anything about the conditions under which the Jews were living in the second century B.C.E. when the stories were written?

3 Why do you think these ancient stories are still popular today?

Members of the congregation at worship in a Progressive synagogue

24   The Writings — Psalms, Proverbs, Job, Ruth

The Book of Psalms has been called the "poetic treasure-house" of the Hebrews. Tradition has it that some, at least, of these great hymns were written by David. They are mainly hymns of praise to God, and are still used regularly for worship, both in synagogues and churches.

"Oh Lord our God, how excellent is your name in all the world! You have set your glory above the heavens."   (Psalm 8, 1)

The Book of Proverbs is a collection of short sayings, traditionally by Solomon, but actually from many sources. Here are some well-known ones:

"A merry heart makes a cheerful face; but sadness at heart breaks the spirit."   (Proverbs 15, 13)

"An angry man stirs up strife; but he that is slow to anger turns away wrath."   (Proverbs 15, 18)

"Train a child in the way he should go; when he is grown up, he will not change."   (Proverbs 22, 6)

The Book of Job is a long debate over the problem of suffering. Several answers are given, but at the end it is still a mystery:

"Then the Lord answered Job out of a whirlwind:

'Who is this that clouds the argument with senseless words? Straighten yourself up and listen, and I will ask you some questions. Where were you when I laid the foundations of the earth? Tell me, if you know. Who decided the measurements of the world? Who marked it out? Who dug the footings, and who laid the cornerstone, when the morning stars sang together, and all the sons of God shouted for joy?' "   (Job 38, 1-7)

The Book of Ruth is set in the period of the Judges, but was written much later, probably in the fourth century B.C.E. It is a *parable* (a story with a point) and tells the story of Ruth, a Moabite woman, and how she was accepted as a wife by Boaz, a Jewish farmer. The point is that God's revelation is for everyone, not just for the Jews. This story is read in the synagogue at the Jewish festival of *Shavuot*.

Boaz watching Ruth gleaning in his field

FOR DISCUSSION

1 Although many of the Psalms are hymns of praise, some are curses against God's enemies. Do you think these Psalms are still used? How do Jews and Christians reconcile these verses with the idea of a God of Mercy?

2 Can you think of any well-known proverbs? Do you know whether they are from the Bible, or some other source? Are they true?

3 What is the meaning of God's answer to Job?

4 The Book of Ruth suggests that God's revelation is for everyone, not just for the Jews. Does it surprise you to find this in the Bible? Do most Jews accept this, do you think?

Part of a page from a medieval manuscript, showing an unusual menorah. The text includes a prayer which is repeated at Hanukah

25 The Maccabees

The Persian King Cyrus took over the Babylonian Empire in 538 B.C.E., and the status of the Jews in Babylon changed from that of exiles to that of foreign residents. They began to return to Jerusalem, and in 520 B.C.E. the rebuilding of the Temple began. Little was achieved, however, until Ezra came and restored the proper forms of worship. The exact date of Ezra's reforms and the completion of the rebuilding of the Temple is not known; it may have been as late as 400 B.C.E.

The difficulties of the Jewish people were by no means over. Alexander the Great conquered the Persian Empire in the fourth century B.C.E., and now the Jews had Greek masters. Not until the reign of Antiochus IV, however, did the troubles really start.

In 168 B.C.E., Antiochus forbade the reading of the Torah and the daily sacrifices in the Temple. Antiochus went so far as to set up an altar to the Greek god Zeus in the Temple and to sacrifice a pig (an unclean animal to the Jews) upon it. This so outraged Jewish feelings that they began a revolt, under the leadership of Judah the Maccabee (the Hammerer). The story of this revolt is found in the two Books of Maccabees, in the *Apocrypha* (writings with hidden meanings).

After three years of fighting, Judah and his men retook the Temple. The story from the Talmud of the miraculous relighting of the Menorah in the Temple is the basis of the Jewish festival of *Hanukah.*

The Book of Daniel dates from this period. Its hidden message to the Jewish reader is to stand firm against Greek tyranny. The fiery furnace (Daniel 3) and the lions' den (Daniel 6) represent the position the Jews found themselves in during the Maccabean War.

A Hanukah menorah

FOR DISCUSSION

1 Why do you think the Jews who returned from exile after 538 B.C.E. failed to achieve any rebuilding for so long?

2 Do you think Antiochus IV deliberately set out to outrage the Jews? If so, why? What was so offensive to the Jews about the sacrifice of a pig in the Temple?

3 Why do you think the Book of Daniel expressed its message in hidden form?

A representation of some of the great sages of Judaism being summoned by their pupils to morning prayers, having spent the night of Passover recounting together the story of the Exodus

26 The Talmud

The Ten Commandments in the Book of Exodus are a summary of the Jewish law, but the next three books of the Torah — Leviticus, Numbers, and Deuteronomy — contain a whole series of laws, covering everyday life, punishment for crime, ritual for worship and sacrifice, and so on. Of course, laws have to be interpreted, and for centuries learned Jewish *rabbis* (teachers) argued about the meaning of the Torah.

Rabbis would memorise the explanations of the Torah that had been taught to them, and pass them on to their own students. One of the most famous rabbis was Akiba, who lived in the second century C.E. when Israel was occupied by the Romans. The Roman Emperor Hadrian forbade the study and teaching of the Torah in 132 C.E., but Akiba carried on teaching. He was captured by the Romans, tortured and killed, but he went on explaining God's words to the anguished onlookers right up to the end.

After this, the Jewish authorities decided that the interpretation of the Torah, which until that time had been passed on by word of mouth, should be written down. The resulting books were known as

Modern Jewish scholars studying the Talmud

the *Mishnah* (Review), edited by the famous Rabbi Judah the Prince. This led to further debate, and many of the arguments were themselves written down word for word. This was called the *Gemara* (Completion).

The process of compiling the Gemara finally came to an end about 500 C.E., when Rabbi Ashee and his pupil Rabina edited a revision of the Mishnah and Gemara which became known as the *Talmud*. This can be translated as "everything within" and it is usually interpreted as "study" or "learning".

FOR DISCUSSION

1   One of the most famous laws of the Torah is "An eye for an eye and a tooth for a tooth" (Exodus 21, 24). How would you interpret this? Do you agree with the principle of "an eye for an eye"?

2   Emperor Hadrian's edict forbidding the study and teaching of the Torah came immediately after an unsuccessful revolt by a Jewish rebel called Bar Kochba. Why do you think Hadrian took this step? What effect do you think the execution of Akiba had upon the Jews?

3   Why do you think the Jews decided that the interpretation of the Torah should be written down?

65

Things to do — Judaism

1   The Tanak, or Old Testament, is made up of a number of different books covering 2000 years of Jewish history. It is really a library of many different kinds of literature: poetry, history, legend, law, philosophy, fiction. Make a list of the thirty-nine books in the Old Testament and decide in which category of literature you would put each book:

NAME OF BOOK	TYPE OF LITERATURE
1 Genesis	Myth and legend? or history?

2 Exodus   ....

If every member of the class makes two model books from the Old Testament (agree on the size — e.g. use matchboxes), you could make your own model Old Testament Library, and arrange it according to the different kinds of literature.

2   Draw a map of the Fertile Crescent, showing Abraham's journey from Ur to Canaan and then to Egypt.

Mountains in the Sinai Desert, where Moses received the Ten Commandments

A street sign of the Ten Commandments in modern Tel Aviv

3　Read the story of Abraham and Isaac, when Abraham thought that God wanted him to sacrifice Isaac (Genesis 22, verses 1-18). Write the story in your own words, as if you were one of their servants.

4　Write out the Ten Commandments, with a sentence or two for each one to explain why it was important and necessary for the Jewish people.

5　Read the story of the crossing of the Red Sea, or Sea of Reeds (Exodus 14, verses 5-31). Write an account of this event as if you were writing it for a newspaper, and give your own theory or explanation of what happened.

6　Read the story of Naboth's vineyard (I Kings 21, verses 1-24). Work out an improvised dramatisation of this story. You will need the following characters: Ahab, Naboth, Jezebel, King Ahab's servants, some elders and nobles of Naboth's city, Elijah, and (off stage) the voice of God.

7　Most of the Old Testament prophets were fearless critics of the kings and rulers of their time, and did not hesitate to speak out against injustice and tyranny in the name of God. Imagine one of the Old Testament prophets — Amos or Isaiah — appearing today. What do you think he would have to say about the politicians and

John the Baptist baptising Christ — a painting by Joachim Patinir

27   The Place of the Old Testament

The prophets of the Old Testament looked forward to a future king, the Messiah, who would be of "the house of Jesse" (Jesse was David's father).

> "A shoot will grow up out of the stump of Jesse, and a branch from his roots. The spirit of the Lord shall be upon him, the spirit of wisdom and understanding, the spirit of ministry and power, the spirit of knowledge and the love of God."   (Isaiah 11, 1-2)

The early Christians soon began to apply these prophecies to Jesus. All the first disciples were Jews, and their only Bible, at first, was the Tanak. Christians today still read these passages and apply them to Jesus, especially at Christmas, the celebration of the birth of Jesus.

One of the greatest difficulties for the early Christians was that the ministry of Jesus, in the eyes of the world, had ended in failure — the shame of execution on the cross. But the Christians soon found a passage in the Tanak which predicted this:

"He was despised and rejected by men; a man of sorrows, well used to grief. As one from whom people turn away their faces, he was ignored, and we did not esteem him . . . He was wounded for our sins, bruised for our wrongdoing. The punishment he bore has brought us pardon, and the scourging he received has set us free."   (Isaiah 53, 3-5)

The stories of the birth of Jesus, written some seventy or eighty years after the event, reflect the understanding which had grown up in the early Church that Jesus was indeed the long-expected Messiah. The angel that appeared to Mary was quite clear about this:

"The Lord God has chosen you, Mary, for a special task. You are to have a son and you must call him Jesus. He is going to be a great man; the people will call him Son of the Most High God. He will be given the throne of David, and will be King of Israel for ever."   (Luke 1, 30-33)

Even the shepherds in the fields were given the same message:

"A baby has been born in Bethlehem who will be the Messiah, the new David you have all been waiting for."   (Luke 2, 11)

John the Baptist, calling people to repentance and baptising them in the river Jordan, is in Christian eyes the last of the Old Testament prophets, the forerunner of the Christ:

Shepherds and their sheep near Bethlehem today

"A lonely voice crying in the wilderness, 'Prepare the way for the Lord'." (Luke 3, 4-5, quoting Isaiah 40, 3)

FOR DISCUSSION

1 Why do you think the passage from Isaiah 53 in the Tanak convinced the early Christians that Jesus was the Messiah?

2 The Gospel writers were not writing eyewitness history but were writing to convert people, to make them believe. If their methods seem to us in some way dubious, does this make Jesus any less significant a figure?

The conversion of Saul — a painting by Tintoretto

28 Early Christian Preaching and Writing

At first, the early Christian Church did not have any writings of its own. The message about Jesus the Messiah was passed on by word of mouth. It is difficult for us to know exactly what the early Christian teaching was, because it has been developed and elaborated by later writers, but it probably contained the claim that Jesus was the Messiah, the anointed one. There is no indication that in their early preaching and teaching the followers of Jesus made any claim that Jesus was the Son of God. This came later, when they were preaching to Gentiles (non-Jews) who did not understand the word "Messiah".

The earliest Christian writings in the New Testament are the letters of Paul. Previously known as Saul, he was a Jew and a Roman citizen, who was at first violently opposed to the Christians. Saul was converted, on the road to Damascus, in a dramatic experience in which he heard Jesus speak to him. He then called himself Paul and became the foremost *Apostle* (one sent out) of the Church, travelling as far as Greece and Rome to spread the good news of Jesus to Jews and Gentiles alike. He established churches in many towns and cities which he visited, and it is his letters to these young churches,

Paul escaping over the walls of Damascus in a basket — a painting in the Chapel of Ananias, Damascus

called the Epistles of Paul, which we find in the Christian New Testament.

The earliest of Paul's letters is probably the one to the Galatians (49 C.E. — just sixteen years after the death of Jesus). This is mainly about the question of non-Jews who became Christians; did they have to become Jews first? Paul thought not:

"For through faith you are all sons of God together with Jesus Christ. Baptised in the name of Jesus, you have put on Jesus like an article of clothing. There is no such thing as Jew or Greek, slave or free man, male or female; you are all one in Jesus Christ."

(Galatians 3, 26-29)

One of the most famous passages in Paul's letters is the chapter about love, in his first letter to the Corinthians (53 C.E.):

"Love is patient; love is kind, and doesn't envy anyone . . .

There are three things that will last for ever: faith, hope, and love. But of these, the greatest is love." (I Corinthians, 13)

FOR DISCUSSION

1 Why is it difficult for us to know the teaching of the early Christian Church?

2 When and why did the early Church start to teach that Jesus was the Son of God? What do you think this means?

3 Why do you think Paul wrote to the churches he had established?

4 In Paul's letter to the Corinthians, what do you think he means by "love"?

Jesus opening the eyes of a man born blind — a painting by Duccio

29 Jesus and the Gospels

Paul's letters said very little about the life of Jesus. He assumed that people knew about Jesus, so he concentrated on explaining what the death and resurrection of Jesus meant. But as the years went by, and the message of Jesus spread further and further away from the places where the events in his life occurred, there was a need for the life and teaching of Jesus to be written down. This is why the Gospels were first written. The Gospel writers are called *evangelists*, from the Greek word meaning "good news". Gospel comes from the Anglo-Saxon "godspel", which means "good tidings".

Even the Gospels, however, are not complete biographies of Jesus. They say very little about what happened to him before he was thirty, concentrating instead on the two or three years that he spent going around teaching and healing. More than half of the Gospels is taken up with the events of the last week in the life of Jesus, leading up to the crucifixion and resurrection.

The first three Gospels — Matthew, Mark and Luke — are called the *Synoptic* Gospels. This means that they are all written from the same point of view (synoptic = seen together). The Gospel of John is very different and is described in Unit 34. Mark was probably written about 65 C.E. It contains sayings and stories told by Jesus, miracle stories, things Jesus did, and an account of the last week of his life — the Passion story (*Passion*, in this sense, means suffering). Matthew was probably written about 75 C.E., and Luke and the Acts of the Apostles about 90 C.E.

The order in which the events related in the Gospels actually happened does not seem to have been particularly important to the evangelists, except that, of course, they all end with the Passion story.

Jesus was born, according to Matthew and Luke, in Bethlehem, near Jerusalem, in the reign of Herod the Great. He was brought up, however, in the town of Nazareth, near Galilee, in northern Palestine. We know very little about his family, except that his father, Joseph, was a carpenter and was descended from David. This was important to the evangelists because they were trying to show that Jesus was the Messiah, the anointed one, the Son of David.

At the age of thirty, Jesus was baptised in the river Jordan, and spent some time alone in the wilderness thinking out what he should do. The evangelists described this period as forty days in which he was tempted by the Devil. He then began a ministry of teaching and healing, mainly around Galilee. This was not unusual; there were many "healers" at this time, who healed people by "casting out demons".

The Gospels describe Jesus as being hugely popular among the common people, except in his home town of Nazareth (Mark 6, 1-6).

FOR DISCUSSION

1 Why did it become necessary for the details of the life and teaching of Jesus to be written down? Why did the evangelists give so little detail of Jesus's family and early life?

2 Why did the evangelists stress the fact that Joseph was descended from King David (Luke 1, 27)?

3 Why do you think Jesus was not accepted in his home town?

The Sermon on the Mount — a painting by Claude Lorrain

30   The Teaching of Jesus

In order to understand the teaching of Jesus, one has to try to get back to the time when Jesus and his disciples were walking around Galilee, teaching and healing. Jesus taught in *parables* — stories with a single, central point, usually about the Kingdom of God. The point of the story was more important than the detail. He used the everyday things and people he could see around him — sheep and shepherds, rich men and poor, fathers and sons, fishermen and farmers:

"One day a farmer was sowing seed for corn, scattering the seed from left to right as he went. Some of the seed fell on a footpath, where the ground was beaten hard; it wasn't there long before the birds came and gobbled it up. Some seed fell on rocky ground, where there was only a thin layer of topsoil; it germinated quickly, but because it had no real roots it withered away in the sun. Some of the seed fell among weeds, which choked it. But some of the seed fell on good soil; it grew strong and tall in the sunshine and yielded a good crop."

(Matthew 13; Mark 4; Luke 8)

Most of his hearers would have seen the point of this story at once, but when the evangelists came to write it down many years later, they added a detailed explanation.

The religious leaders of the time, the Scribes and Pharisees, used to object to the way that Jesus mixed with people they regarded as sinners: drop-outs, drunkards, prostitutes and the like. Jesus answered them with this story:

"If a shepherd has a hundred sheep and finds one of them is missing, what does he do? Why, he leaves the ninety-nine in a field and goes off to look for the missing one. And how pleased he is when he finds it! He lifts it on to his shoulders and carries it home, calling out to his friends and neighbours to celebrate with him — he has found his missing sheep. In just the same way, there is more joy in heaven over one sinner who repents than over ninety-nine righteous people who do not need to repent."

(Matthew 18; Luke 15)

FOR DISCUSSION

1   What do you think Jesus meant by the Kingdom of God?

2   Why did the evangelists think it was necessary to explain the parable of the sower? What was their explanation?

3   What reason did Jesus give for spending his time with "sinners"?

4   Discuss other well-known parables of Jesus that you have read or heard, such as the Prodigal Son (Matthew 21) or the Good Samaritan (Luke 10). What do you think is the central point of each of these stories?

The Entry into Jerusalem — a painting by Duccio

31 The Entry into Jerusalem

The turning-point of the Synoptic Gospels is an incident that happened when Jesus and the disciples went to the north of Palestine to Mount Hermon.

"Jesus asked the disciples who people thought he was.

'Some say John the Baptist reborn,' they replied. 'Others say Elijah, or another of the prophets.'

'And what about you?' asked Jesus. 'Who do you think I am?'

'You are the Messiah,' replied Peter.

From then on, Jesus began to teach the disciples that the Messiah would not be a great king like David, who would drive out the Romans, but one who would suffer and die, like the Suffering Servant in Isaiah." (Mark 8, Matthew 16, Luke 9)

Jesus made up his mind to go to Jerusalem, although he knew that the Jewish authorities wanted him dead.

He entered the city riding a donkey, which the evangelists interpret as a fulfilment of the prophecy of Zechariah:

"Here is your King, who comes to you riding upon an ass, in peace and gentleness." (Matthew 21, 4-5, quoting Zechariah 9)

It was the Feast of Pesach (Passover), and all the crowds were chanting the words of the psalms to greet the Passover pilgrims:

"Blessed are those who come in the name of the Lord; blessings on the kingdom of David." (Matthew 21, 9, quoting Psalm 118, 26)

The first thing Jesus did on entering Jerusalem was to go to the Temple. Here he found the Court of the Gentiles crowded with pilgrims, buying lambs, goats and pigeons for sacrifice. They had to pay in special temple-money, and there were money-changers everywhere, changing Greek or Roman coins into the special temple coinage. Jesus was appalled.

"'Listen to me!' he cried out. 'Have you not read in the prophet Isaiah, "My house shall be called a house of prayer for all nations?" You have turned it into a robbers' cave!' He strode over to the tables of the money-changers and began overturning them, scattering money in all directions." (Matthew 21, Luke 19)

From then on, the Jewish religious authorities — chief priests, Pharisees and lawyers — began to try and find a way to have Jesus killed.

FOR DISCUSSION

1   How did Jesus's understanding of the role of the Messiah differ from that which people were expecting?

2   What was the significance of Jesus entering Jerusalem seated on an ass? Do you think the crowds who were cheering the arrival of the Passover pilgrims understood this symbolic action of Jesus, or is this something the evangelists put in to make a point about the kind of Messiah Jesus was to be?

3   Why was Jesus so appalled by the money-changers in the Temple? Why did his action so upset the Temple authorities?

The Garden of Gethsemane today

32   The Crucifixion

Jesus and the disciples went to a private room to celebrate the Passover meal together. It should not be forgotten that they were Jews and observed all the Jewish festivals. During the meal, Jesus broke bread and took the cup of wine, and told his disciples that every time they did this, they should do so in memory of him. Christians remember this today in the celebration called Eucharist or Holy Communion.

After the meal, Jesus and the disciples went to a garden called the Garden of Gethsemane on the slopes of the Mount of Olives.

Jesus, knowing what lay ahead of him, prayed desperately that God should show him another way, but to no avail. Judas Iscariot arrived at the head of a column of Temple police, and Jesus was arrested and taken to the High Priest's house. The hastily-convened trial that followed (Matthew 26, Luke 22) does not appear to have been conducted according to the strict Jewish regulations, and may have been a private examination rather than a trial.

In reply to the High Priest's direct question, "Are you the Messiah?", Jesus replied quoting Psalm 110, verse 1, and Daniel 7, 13:

> "The words are yours; but I tell you this: you will see a son of man sitting on the right hand of God, and coming on the clouds of heaven."   (Matthew 26, 64; Luke 22, 69)

That was enough for the Jewish authorities. They did not have the

The Crucifixion — part of the altar-piece at Issenheim by Matthias Grünewald

power to exact the death penalty, however, so they brought Jesus before Pontius Pilate, the Roman Governor, on the trumped-up charge of claiming to be the King of the Jews. It was treason to make such a claim, and Jesus was condemned to death by crucifixion.

Crucifixion was a cruel, lingering form of execution used widely by the Romans. Jesus had to carry his cross to the place of execution, where he was nailed to it and left hanging there to die. According to Matthew, Jesus cried out from the cross just before he died: "My God, my God, why have you forsaken me?"

FOR DISCUSSION

1 When Jesus prayed to God in the Garden of Gethsemane to be spared the cruel death which he knew awaited him, he ended his prayer, "Nevertheless, not my will, but yours, be done." What does this tell us about the Christian attitude to prayer?

2 Why did Pilate agree to have Jesus put to death?

The Garden Tomb, Jerusalem

33   The Resurrection

After Jesus had died, Joseph of Arimathea, a member of the Jewish council who was sympathetic towards Jesus, obtained permission to take the body for burial. It was late on Friday, and the Sabbath was about to start, so there was only time to take the body to the tomb and leave it there.

Early on Sunday morning, some of the women who were followers of Jesus went to the tomb with ointment and spices to prepare the body for burial. When they came to the tomb, they found to their astonishment that the stone over the entrance had been rolled away and the tomb was empty. The evangelists differ on what happened next: Mark says a young man was sitting in the tomb; Matthew says an angel was seated on the stone; Luke says two men in dazzling garments appeared. The message to the women was clear: Jesus had been raised from the dead (Matthew 28, Mark 16, Luke 24).

Inside the Garden Tomb

The women ran back to tell the disciples, who thought the women were hysterical and would not believe them. Later that day, however, Jesus appeared to two disciples on the road to Emmaus (Luke 24) and subsequently appeared to them all.

Seven weeks after these events, the disciples were meeting together to celebrate the festival of Pentecost when the whole house was filled with a sound like a gale-force wind. As they looked at one another, they saw that every one of them was somehow transformed. When the disciples tried to describe it afterwards, they said it looked as if flames of fire were resting on each of them. They knew, suddenly, that the "Spirit of God" which Jesus had promised had come to them. Full of confidence, they started to go out and preach the good news of Jesus Christ to all who would listen.

Whatever happened in those mysterious early days of the Christian Church, something changed the disciples from a terrified, demoralised group into a band of men prepared to stand up for what they believed. Within a very short time they had hundreds of followers, and one of the elected *deacons* (organisers), Stephen, was brought before the Jewish council, found guilty of blasphemy, and stoned to death (Acts 7). One of the witnesses to this was Saul, who became Paul. Peter himself was to die for his faith, but the church that he founded in Rome was to become the centre of Christendom.

FOR DISCUSSION

1 Why did the body of Jesus have to be left unprepared for burial on Friday night?

2 The evangelists disagree about the details of what happened when the women found the empty tomb. Does this make it more, or less, likely to be true?

3 What do you think happened at that first Pentecost after the death of Jesus? What is meant by the "Spirit of God"?

The Raising of Lazarus — a painting by Benozzo Gozzoli

34   The Gospel of John

The Gospel of John was written in a style quite different from the other three gospels. It was probably written about 100 C.E., seventy years after the death of Jesus, and there is a tradition that the author was John, disciple and close friend of Jesus. The Gospel is linked with Ephesus, where John is believed to have ended his days.

John took the traditional elements of the ministry of Jesus and used them freely, altering the order in the light of his overall understanding of the significance of Jesus. The gospel has a very formal structure. It opens like this:

"In the beginning, there was the Word. The Word was with God, and the Word was God . . ."   (John 1, 1)

This is followed by the story of John the Baptist. Then the public ministry of Jesus is recorded in sections, each beginning with a sign or miracle and followed by a long explanation. Next, there is a long conversation between Jesus and the Father, God, and the gospel ends with the Passion story.

John includes many stories and miracles not recorded in the other gospels, but he uses them to explain his beliefs about Jesus — they are "signs". He often speaks of the new quality of life Jesus brought, which he calls "eternal life". To explain this concept, he tells the story of the raising of Lazarus:

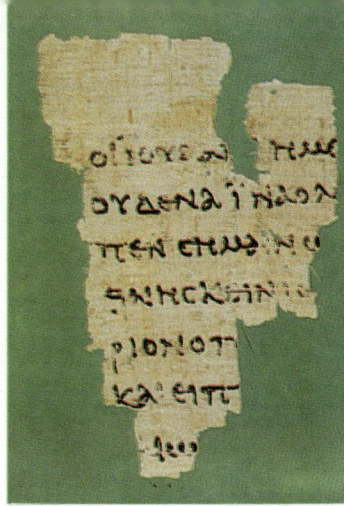

A fragment of early manuscript of the Gospel of St John

"Jesus had some friends who lived in the village of Bethany, near Jerusalem. There were two sisters, Martha and Mary, and their brother Lazarus. One day Lazarus became seriously ill, and his sisters sent for Jesus in the hope that he could cure him. But by the time Jesus arrived, Lazarus had been dead for four days and was already laid in a tomb.

Martha went out to meet Jesus. 'Master, if only you had been here, my brother would not have died,' she said.

'Don't be afraid,' Jesus said to her. 'Anyone who has faith in me, even if he dies, will live again. Do you believe this?'

'Master, I do,' Martha replied. 'I know now that you are the Messiah.'

They went to the tomb, and Jesus ordered them to roll back the stone.

'Father, I thank you,' he prayed. 'I know you always hear me, but I am speaking for the sake of the people who are listening, so that they should know you sent me.' Then he faced the mouth of the cave.

'Lazarus, come out!' he called, and Lazarus walked out of the cave, still wrapped in the grave clothes.

'Free him of his wrappings, and let him go,' Jesus commanded."

(John 11)

FOR DISCUSSION

1 John used the word "sign" rather than "miracle" for the supernatural events he described. Do you think John meant the reader to take these "signs" literally?

2 What do you think John meant by "eternal life"?

Christ in Revelation, from an early fourteenth-century English manuscript

35 Later Epistles and Revelation

Not all the letters in the New Testament which bear Paul's name were written by him personally. They are in his style and continue his teaching, but seem to refer to events and conditions which happened after his death.

The early parts of the New Testament, such as Paul's letters to the Galatians, the Thessalonians and the Corinthians, were all written at a time when the Christians were expecting the end of the world at any moment:

"This is the word of the Lord: we who live until the Lord returns will not take precedence over those who have died. At the word of command, when the trumpet sounds, the Lord will come down from heaven; those Christians who have died will rise up, then we who are alive will join them . . ."

(I Thessalonians 4, 15-18. About 50 C.E.)

By contrast, letters such as those to Timothy and Titus may date from a later period, when the Church had existed for some time and leaders such as Timothy or Titus were beginning to take on the duties which would later be called those of a bishop.

The New Testament also contains shorter letters said to be by the apostles James, Peter, John and Jude. It is now thought that these belong to a later period, probably the second century C.E. The first letter of John develops the idea that God is Love:

"God is love; anyone who lives in love lives in God, and God lives in him." (I John 4, 16)

The last book of the New Testament, Revelation, is quite different from the rest. It probably dates from about 95 C.E., when the seven Christian Churches were being persecuted by the Roman authorities. It is full of symbols and coded messages:

"I saw seven golden standing lamps, and among them a figure like a son of man, wearing a long robe, with a golden belt around his shoulders . . . In his right hand he held seven stars, a sharp two-edged sword was in his mouth . . . The seven stars are the angels of the seven churches, and the seven lamps are the seven churches." (Revelation 1, 12, 13, 16, 20)

Revelation is the kind of literature known as *apocalyptic* (to do with the last things, the end of the world).

FOR DISCUSSION

1   Why did the early Christians expect the end of the world to come soon? Why did they gradually change their views?

2   Why do you think the writer of Revelation used coded language?

ſt thereof, | ſant to the eyes, and a tree to be deſired | he ſhould ſay
, Jt is not | to get knowledge)tooke of ȳ fruit there⸗ | God doeth
himſelfe a⸗ | of, and did * eat, and gaue alſo to her huſ⸗ | forbid you
lpe ‡ meete | band with her, and he f did eat. | eate of ȳ fru
ned of the | **7** Then the eyes of them both were | ſaue ȳ kno
and euery | opened, and they g knew that they were | eth that if ye
ght [them] | naked, and they ſewed figge tree leaues | ſhould eat th
would call | together, ⁊ made them ſelues ‡ breeches. | of, ye ſhould
n named ȳ | **8** ¶ Afterward they heard the boyce | like to him,
me thereof. | of the Lord God walking in ȳ garden in | Ecclus. 25, 2
ue names | the ‖coole of the day, and the man ⁊ his | 1. tim. 2, 14.
of the hea⸗ | wife h hid them ſelues from the preſence | f Not ſonſ
ld : but for | of the Lord God among the trees of the | to pleaſe hi
garden. | wife, as mo
9 But the Lord God called to ȳ man, | by ambition

The extract at Genesis 3, 7, from which the 'Breeches Bible' got its name

36 The Translation of the Bible

The Old Testament was originally written in Hebrew, although early in the Christian era a Greek version called the *Septuagint* was widely known. The New Testament was written in Greek (apart from a few words of Aramaic), but was translated into other languages (Latin, Syriac, Egyptian) quite early on. Manuscripts from the second and third centuries C.E. are rare and fragmentary, and contain a number of minor differences which cause problems for scholars.

In England, as in most of Christendom, the earliest Christians would have used a Latin Bible. One of the earliest Latin translations was that of Jerome, whose text was called the *Vulgate* because it was written in the everyday Latin of the time (382 C.E.).

The first complete translation of the New Testament into English was by John Wycliffe in the late fourteenth century C.E. Printing started in the late fifteenth century, whereupon the Bible became more readily available to ordinary people, and as a result of the

Reformation and the demand from lay people (i.e. non-priests), William Tyndale's translation of the New Testament into English was printed and published in 1525 C.E.

Following this, Miles Coverdale produced the first complete Bible in English in 1535 C.E.. His translation shows some dependence on Tyndale's. Coverdale's translation of the Psalms was used in Thomas Cranmer's Book of Common Prayer. From this time, an increasing number of versions of the Bible began to circulate. In 1560 C.E., the *Geneva Bible* was published, and went into ninety-six editions over the following hundred years. This is also known as the *Breeches Bible*, because in Genesis 3, 7 it states that Adam and Eve "made themselves breeches".

The *Bishops' Bible* of 1568, published by a committee chaired by Archbishop Parker, was never very popular, but became the basis of the *Authorised* (or *King James*) *Bible* of 1611, still widely used today and much loved for its dignified, solemn English.

The Authorised Version was revised in the 1880s, and this Revised Version (although it never replaced the Authorised Version) is still used as one of the most accurate renderings of the earliest available manuscripts.

There have been many modern translations in English in the twentieth century, J. B. Phillips's being one of the best known. This is a very free translation, but widely used because it is so readable. In 1970 the complete *New English Bible* was published, and at the same time the Catholic Church published the *Jerusalem Bible*.

FOR DISCUSSION

1   Before Wycliffe's translation of the Bible into English, ordinary people in England could not read the Bible. Why do you think many leaders — noblemen and bishops — were opposed to Wycliffe's translation?

2   Many people still prefer the Authorised (King James) Version of the Bible to any of the more modern translations. Why do you think this is?

3   Why do you think the minor differences between early manuscripts of the New Testament cause so much difficulty to scholars and translators?

Things to do — Christianity

1 Imagine you are having a discussion where you are trying to convince someone else about something you believe in very strongly, but which is difficult or impossible to prove — for example, that the latest fashion is out of this world and you just could not go to the disco in anything else. List the arguments you would use. Then, working in pairs, try to convince each other.

2 Read the story of the conversion of Saul (Acts of the Apostles 9, verses 1-30). Working in groups, dramatise and act out the story. You will need the following characters: Saul; the High Priest; Saul's companions; Ananias; the voice of the Lord; Jews in the synagogue at Damascus; Barnabas; and some of the apostles (e.g. Peter, James, John).

3 Read the accounts of the birth of Jesus in Matthew 1 and 2, and Luke 1 and 2. Hold a formal class debate on the motion "This

The three kings presenting their gifts to the infant Jesus — an illustration from an early English manuscript

Part of a page from a medieval manuscript, showing the resurrection of Jesus

house believes that the Virgin Birth of Jesus is a historical fact and not mere symbolism."

4   Read one of the well-known parables of Jesus, e.g. the Good Samaritan (Luke 10, verses 25-37), or the Prodigal Son (Luke 15, verses 11-32). Write a modern version of one of these parables, using a present-day setting.

5   Imagine you are a newspaper reporter writing for the *Jerusalem Herald* at the time of Jesus. Write an account of the triumphal entry of Jesus into Jerusalem and his actions in the Temple.

6   Read the different accounts of the resurrection of Jesus (Matthew 28, Mark 16, Luke 24, John 20). List the arguments for and against the historical truth of the resurrection. Ask a number of church-going Christians what they believe about the resurrection of Jesus, and what are the grounds for their belief. As a class, list all the answers you have obtained. What are the most common answers? What do *you* believe?

7   The writer of the fourth Gospel, John, uses signs and symbols which carry a deeper significance than their outward appearance. What is the significance of the story of the raising of Lazarus?

Paul preaching in Athens — a painting by Raphael

8   Imagine yourself living during the period 35-60 C.E., when Paul is on his missionary journeys and the good news of Jesus Christ is beginning to spread, but before any Gospels have been written. You are a Jew, and you and a group of your friends were converted to Christianity by Paul when he visited your town some months ago. Describe what happens when you receive a letter from Paul.

9   Select a well-known passage from the New Testament, about one chapter in length, and read it carefully until you are quite familiar with it. Then close the Bible and write the chapter in your own words, in modern, everyday English. As a class, read each other's efforts and decide whether or not these new versions are easier to understand than the originals.

Islam

Islam means submission to God's will. Followers of Islam, called Muslims, believe that Islam began with the creation of man, and that God's final revelation to man was given to Muhammad, the last of the prophets, in the seventh century C.E. When he received God's revelation, Muhammad began to recite the verses which later became part of the Qur'an.

Less than a hundred years after Muhammad's death in 632 C.E., his followers had conquered many of the countries of the Mediterranean, including Spain, Turkey, Persia, Arabia, part of France, and much of North Africa.

This section follows the life of Muhammad and the leaders of Islam who succeeded him (known as Caliphs), and examines the central book of Islam, the Qur'an, and the sayings of the Prophet, called the Hadith.

The Black Stone, encrusted with silver and set into the walls of the Ka'aba

37   Muhammad

The prophet Muhammad was born in the year 570 C.E., in the city of Mecca, in Arabia. From the age of eight he lived with his uncle, Abu Talib, as his father and mother and his grandfather had all died.

Abu Talib was a trader whose dealings by camel caravan took him to many countries, and Muhammad spent his youth in his uncle's business. From then on Muhammad grew increasingly dissatisfied with the society in which he lived. Arabia at that time was very unsettled. The tribes were constantly at war with each other, moral standards were low, and people worshipped idols. Muhammad stood out from the rest. He did not gamble or drink, and would never take part in idol worship.

When he was twenty-five, a business woman called Khadija, the widow of a wealthy merchant, asked Muhammad to take charge of a caravan of her goods to be taken to Syria. Muhammad proved to be as reliable as his reputation, and before long he and Khadija were married. She later became the first convert to Islam.

Muhammad placing the stone in the thoub — from an Arabic manuscript

In Mecca there was a black stone, probably a meteorite, which for hundreds of years had been worshipped as holy. It was built into a cubic stone structure called the *Ka'aba*. The people of Mecca decided to rebuild the Ka'aba as the stonework was cracking. All went well until the time came to lift the black stone back into place; then the different tribes fell out over who should have the honour of lifting it. They decided to ask the first person who came by to choose. This happened to be Muhammad. He called for a *thoub*, a large sheet of cloth, put it under the stone, and told one man from each tribe to take hold of the edge of the thoub and lift. This meant they all had the honour of replacing the stone, and a possible war was averted.

Muhammad used to retire to a cave in the mountains from time to time, to meditate and pray to God. One night, during Ramadan, Muhammad was in the cave when he heard a voice telling him to read. The command came three times, until Muhammad protested that he could not read. Then he was told to recite these words:

"Read! in the name of the Lord who created man out of a mere clot of blood, Read! the Lord is most generous, He who taught by the Pen, taught men that which they knew not." (Qur'an 96, 1-5)

These were the first words of God (called *Allah* in Arabic) spoken to Muhammad through the angel Gabriel, and this came to be known as the Night of Power.

FOR DISCUSSION

1   What sort of person do you imagine Muhammad to have been?

2   After the Night of Power, what do you think was going through Muhammad's mind? How do you think Khadija reacted when he came home and told her about his experience?

Medina today

38 The Spread of Islam

Khadija took Muhammad to see her cousin Wareqah, a Christian who had studied both the Jewish and the Christian scriptures. He told them that a Prophet was expected, and that the message Muhammad had received meant that he would be that Prophet. A short time later, Muhammad heard the voice again; he was told to go and warn the people that they should worship God, and God only.

Muhammad began to preach in Mecca, and soon had many followers. The main tribe of Mecca, the Quraish, realised that Muhammad's teaching would upset the social order because he opposed the worship of idols, stood up for the rights of the poor, and claimed that slaves were equal to their masters. The Quraish consequently opposed Muhammad, and began to punish his followers.

96

At that time, many Arabs used to make a pilgrimage to Mecca to worship at the Ka'aba. In the year 620 C.E. a group of pilgrims from Medina, some three hundred kilometres to the north of Mecca, heard Muhammad preach and were very impressed by his message. The following year they came again, and a trusted follower of Muhammad went back to Medina with them to spread the message.

By now, conditions for the Muslims in Mecca were getting worse, and when, in 622 C.E., Muhammad received an invitation to go to Medina and take a leading role there, he gladly accepted. He and many of his followers migrated to Medina, which soon became a Muslim city ruled by the Prophet. This migration, known as the *Hijrah*, became such an important event in Muslim history that it was made the first year of the Muslim calendar.

Over the next eight years, the hostility of the Meccans to the Muslims in Medina grew, and there were a number of battles between the Quraish and the followers of Muhammad. Eventually, in 630 C.E., Muhammad and his army retook Mecca in a bloodless victory, and the people of Mecca accepted Muhammad as the Prophet. The idols in the city were destroyed and Mecca became the centre of Islam.

The Prophet died in 632 C.E., and was buried in Medina, the city that first accepted him. According to the Qur'an, Muhammad was a man chosen by God to be a prophet and an apostle, one sent by God to the people:

"Muhammad is no more than an apostle; there were many apostles before him . . ." (Qur'an 3, 144)

FOR DISCUSSION

1 Why did the Quraish oppose Muhammad?

2 Why does the Muslim calendar date from 622 C.E.?

3 Why do you think the people of Medina wanted Muhammad to come and take a leading role in their community?

The opening spread of a decorated Qur'an

39   The Qur'an

The Qur'an is a collection of the messages, some short, some long, which Muhammad received from God through the angel Gabriel. It is divided into 114 chapters, called *suras*. The Qur'an was not written down during the Prophet's lifetime, and Muhammad himself could neither read nor write. He is referred to in the Qur'an as "the illiterate Prophet known to the (Jewish) Torah and the (Christian) Gospel" (Qur'an 7, 157). Many of the Prophet's close followers knew parts of the Qur'an by heart, and after his death in 632 C.E. they began to write it down in Arabic.

The word *Qur'an* comes from an Arabic word meaning "to read" or "to recite". The shorter passages in the Qur'an are believed to be from the early years of the Prophet's ministry, 610 – 622 C.E.; the longer sections date from the period when he and his followers were in Medina.

The Qur'an teaches that God chose many prophets through the ages to guide mankind to himself:

"You shall say that we believe in God, and the revelation given to us, and to Abraham, to Isma'il, Isaac and Jacob, to the tribes, and given to Moses and Jesus, and that given to all the prophets from their God. We see no difference between any of them, and we submit to God, in Islam." (Qur'an 2, 136)

The fundamental principle of Islam is the belief in one God:

"In the name of God, the merciful, the giver of mercy, say: he is God, the one and only God, who stands alone, upon whom everything else depends. Nobody made him, and he has no son, there is nothing you can compare him to."

(Qur'an 112)

A very early copy of the Qur'an, believed to date from the time of Uthman

As part of this belief in one God and submission to him, the Muslim says many times a day:

"Bismil-Lahil-Rahaminr-Raheem."

(In the name of God, most Gracious, most Merciful.)

This is said on waking and before sleeping, during prayers, when starting work, and as a grace before meals.

A Muslim also calls upon God in prayer, using the ninety-nine beautiful names, or qualities, of God in the Qur'an. To help in repeating all the names without mistake, a Muslim uses a string of ninety-nine beads, called *misbaha* in Arabic or *tasbir* in Turkish.

The Qur'an also teaches belief in a Day of Judgement:

"Whoever does good shall have ten times as much, but whoever does evil shall be recompensed with evil, although they shall not be dealt with unjustly." (Qur'an 6, 161)

FOR DISCUSSION

1 What does the Qur'an teach about the prophets of Judaism?

2 The Qur'an teaches that Jesus was a prophet, but that he was a man, not God. How does this compare with early Christian teaching?

3 What is the main belief that Islam has in common with Judaism and Christianity?

The Dome of the Rock, Jerusalem

40 The Rightly-Guided Caliphs

After the death of the Prophet, the Muslim community was led for the next thirty years by four men in turn, who had all been close companions of Muhammad during his ministry. These men were called *Caliphs* (successors).

The first was Abu Bakr, who was Muhammad's closest friend, one of the first to believe when Muhammad began to hear the revelations of God through Gabriel. Abu Bakr led the Muslims from 632 to 634 C.E., during which time he collected together the revelations of the Prophet to form the Qur'an.

The second Caliph was Umar, from 634 to 644 C.E. This period saw the spread of Islam into Syria, Iraq and Egypt, and Umar was notably fair and generous in his treatment of Jews and Christians in these countries. He protected their synagogues and churches, and refused to compel them to convert to Islam.

From 644 to 656 C.E., Muhammad's son-in-law Uthman was Caliph. During this time, an authoritative version of the Qur'an was written, and copies were sent to the major Muslim cities. The Qur'an has remained unchanged from that day.

The fourth Caliph was Ali, a cousin of the Prophet, who was married to Fatima, Muhammad's youngest daughter. Ali had been a close friend and adviser of the three earlier Caliphs, and he took over after Uthman was assassinated. Ali ruled from 656 to 661 C.E. He also was assassinated, and after his death Islam never again had one undisputed leader.

An early Persian painting showing Muhammad riding to heaven on Buraq

One of the earliest Muslim places of worship was the Dome of the Rock, on the site of Herod's Temple in Jerusalem. A mosque was first built there in 638 C.E. by Caliph Umar, although the present building dates back to 687 C.E. in the time of Abd al Malek. Although the Dome of the Rock is also known as the Mosque of Umar, it is not really a mosque but a shrine, built over the sacred rock from which Muhammad is said to have ascended to heaven.

The Qur'an relates that when Muhammad was under increasing pressure from the Meccans, the angel Gabriel came to him in the night and took him to a fabulous horse with wings, called Buraq. Riding on this creature, Muhammad was taken from Mecca to Mount Moriah in Jerusalem. From there, he ascended into the Seven Heavens, where he met the earlier prophets Abraham, Moses and Jesus, and was commanded by God to begin the practice of daily prayer which became so important to Muslims.

FOR DISCUSSION

1   Why do you think the Muslim community chose close associates of the Prophet as the first four Caliphs?

2   Why did it become necessary for the Qur'an to be written down?

3   Why do you think that after the fourth Caliph the Muslims were never again able to unite under one leader?

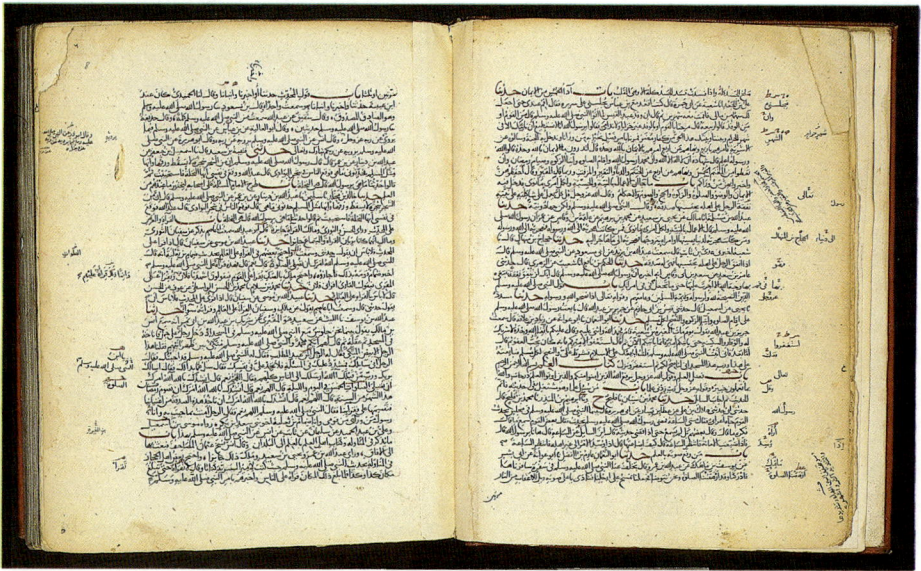

A manuscript Hadith, dating from the fifteenth century C.E.

41   The Hadith

In addition to the Qur'an, which is the main source of rules for behaviour and conduct for the Muslim, there is also the *Sunna*, which means form or way. The Sunna is based on sayings of the prophet Muhammad. Although it is not as authoritative as the Qur'an, because that, to the Muslim, is the revealed word of God, the Sunna is nevertheless an important secondary source of Islamic law.

The Sunna includes the *Hadith*, the sayings of Muhammad. These were written down after his death and collected together by leading Muslims. There are numerous Hadiths, the most widely used being the collections made by Bukhari and Muslim ibn al-Hajjaj.

The Hadith is used to explain the Qur'an and give examples of what it means. For example, the payment of *zakat* (a tax for charity) is laid down by the Qur'an.

The Hadith goes into much more detail about the Prophet's own practice of charity, and what he said on the subject. Details are given of minimum amounts of gold and silver, below which zakat need not be paid; the minimum number of camels on which zakat is payable (five); the amount of zakat to be paid on a proportion of crops grown on land watered by rain (one-tenth) or by wells (one-twentieth), and so on.

Similarly, the Qur'an instructs believers to purify themselves by *wudu* (washing) before worship:

"When you get up to pray, wash your face and hands up to the elbows, and your feet to the ankles . . ." (Qur'an 5, 6)

The Hadith gives details of how the Prophet performed his ablutions:

"He sent for water and poured it over his hands, washed his hands twice, then rinsed his mouth and sniffed water into his nose three times, then washed his face three times; then he washed his hands up to the elbow twice, wiped his head with both his hands . . . then he washed his feet."

Muslims washing before worship

(Hadith of Bukhari, 4, 38)

The study of the Qur'an and the Hadith is an important part of the *Shari'a* ("highway" of God's commands for life).

FOR DISCUSSION

1 Why do Muslims draw a distinction between the Qur'an and the Hadith? Which do they regard as the more authoritative?

2 Why is washing before worship so important to a Muslim?

3 What are the similarities and differences between the Shari'a of Islam and the "ways" of other religions you have studied, e.g. the yogas of Hinduism, the Jain path, and the "Middle Way" of the Buddha?

Things to do — Islam

1 Working in groups, dramatise the incident when Muhammad settled the argument about who should have the honour of lifting the black stone back into place in the rebuilt Ka'aba. You could use a coat for the cloth and a satchel or bag for the stone.

2 Imagine you are one of the leaders of the Quraish tribe in Mecca when Muhammad starts to speak out against idol worship. Prepare a speech to give to your fellow leaders, warning them of the consequences if Muhammad is not stopped.

3 Compare the Muslim belief in the Day of Judgement (Qur'an 6, 161) with the Christian belief as expressed in the parable of the Sheep and the Goats (Matthew 25, verses 31-46).

4 Imagine you are a Christian or a Jew living in Jerusalem in the year 638 C.E. Write a letter to a friend, describing the Muslim occupation of the city and the building of the Dome of the Rock on Mount Moriah.

5 Question 3 in Unit 41 asks you to compare the Shari'a of Islam with the "ways" of other religions. When you have had a discussion about this, make a classroom chart of the similarities and differences:

Central features, e.g.:	Shari'a of Islam	Yogas of Hinduism	Jain ford or path	Buddhist Middle Way
Belief in one God				
Extreme asceticism				
etc.				

Sikhism

Sikhism is the most recent of the religions covered in this book. It has much more in common with Hinduism than with Judaism, Christianity or Islam. It began in the Punjab (North-West India) in the fifteenth century C.E., and twelve million of the fourteen million or so Sikhs in the world still live in that region.

The founder of Sikhism was Guru Nanak (1469-1539 C.E.) and the sacred writing of the Sikhs is called the Adi Granth, or the Guru Granth Sahib. The name *Sikh* comes from the Sanskrit word for disciple, and was used to describe the followers of Guru Nanak.

This section deals with the lives of Nanak and his contemporary, Kabir, the nine Gurus who followed Guru Nanak, and the Guru Granth Sahib, the sacred book of the Sikhs.

Guru Nanak

42   Kabir and Nanak

By the fifteenth century C.E., there were many *bhakti* (holy men and poets, bhakti = devotion) who went about India singing their songs of praise. By this time there was also a strong Muslim tradition in India, and the songs of the Muslim *sufis* (mystics) must have sounded very similar to those of the Hindu bhakti tradition.

One of these holy men was Kabir (1440-1518 C.E.), who devoted his life to trying to reconcile Hinduism and Islam. He was born a Muslim, but seems to have found no difficulty in worshipping in the Hindu tradition. Over five hundred of Kabir's hymns have found their way into the Sikh Bible, the Adi Granth, and a small sect of Kabir's followers still exists.

Nanak, the founder of Sikhism, was born in 1469 C.E. in Talwandi, near Lahore in the Punjab. For several centuries, this had been an area where Hinduism and Islam mingled, and Nanak was born a Hindu in a Muslim village. He seems to have been a dreamy, unworldly youth, and at the age of thirty he had an experience which changed his life.

He was bathing one morning in the river on his way to work, and apparently just disappeared. Three days later he reappeared at the same spot, spent a day in silence, then went home and gave away all his possessions. What had happened in the missing three days? Nanak declared that he had seen a vision of God, that God had given him a cup of nectar to drink and told him to go into the world to pray, to teach others how to pray, and to preach that Hindu and Muslim are one. In response to the divine command, Nanak spoke the words known as the *Mool Mantra* (Perfect Words), the opening section of the morning prayer still said daily by all devout Sikhs:

> "There is one God. He is the supreme Truth. He, the creator, is without fear and without hate. He, the omnipresent, fills the whole Universe. He was not born, nor does he die to be born again. By his grace shall you worship him. Before Time began there was Truth. When Time began to turn the world He was the Truth. Even now, He is the Truth. Truth will last forever."

FOR DISCUSSION

1   How would you account for Nanak's three-day disappearance?

2   Can you see any similarities between the Mool Mantra and the teaching about God in other religions? (See, for example, the Gospel of John, the Qur'an, and the Bhagavad Gita.)

The River Ganges at Benares today

43 The Life of Nanak

After his crisis experience, which is believed to have taken place in 1499 C.E., Nanak set out with his friend Mardana, a musician, to live the life of a wandering *guru* (teacher). Over the next twenty years, they travelled widely in India, Tibet, Sri Lanka, and the Middle East, with Nanak preaching the message of God, the True Name, and singing his hymns of praise, accompanied by Mardana.

To emphasise the unity of Hindu and Muslim, Nanak wore a mixture of Hindu and Muslim clothes. Wherever he went, he tried to set up groups of Sikhs to carry on after he left. Nanak and Mardana even made the traditional Muslim pilgrimage to Mecca. There is a story that on their journey, they slept one night in a mosque, and

Nanak went to sleep with his feet pointing towards the Ka'aba. The *mullah* (Muslim leader) was very offended, as this was disrespectful to Allah, and he shook Nanak awake.

"Servant of God, you have put your feet towards the Ka'aba, the house of God," he said. "Why have you done such a thing?"

"Then turn my feet in some direction where there is no God," Nanak replied.

In the last fifteen years of his life, Nanak settled down in the Punjab village of Kartarpur, where he became the Guru to a growing community of Sikhs. The main theme of Guru Nanak's teaching was "God, the True Name", which was his way of trying to overcome the limitations of Hindu names such as Rama or Siva, and the Muslim name for God, Allah.

Nanak never tired of criticising meaningless rituals in religion. Sikh tradition relates that when he visited the Hindu sacred river, the Ganges, he saw Hindu pilgrims standing in the river throwing water towards the rising sun as an offering to their dead ancestors. He immediately began to throw water in the opposite direction.

"What are you doing that for?" asked the curious bystanders.

"I am watering my fields at home in the Punjab," he replied.

"Don't be silly," they scoffed. "The Punjab is much too far away!"

"If these men can throw water to Heaven, surely I can send some to my home village!" replied the Guru.

FOR DISCUSSION

1   What is the point of the story about Nanak and the direction of the Ka'aba?

2   Why was so much of Nanak's teaching devoted to God, the True Name?

3   What do you think was the Hindu reaction to Nanak's criticism of their religious rituals? If Guru Nanak were alive today and visited Britain, which religious practices do you think he would criticise?

Guru Nanak and the other nine Gurus of the Sikhs

44 The Ten Gurus

When Nanak knew he was dying, he named one of his followers as his successor, and gave him the name Angad, perhaps best translated as "my right-hand man". There were ten Gurus altogether:

1	Nanak	died 1539 C.E.
2	Angad	died 1552 C.E.
3	Amar Das	died 1574 C.E.
4	Ram Das	died 1581 C.E.
5	Arjan	died 1606 C.E.
6	Hargobind	died 1644 C.E.
7	Har Rai	died 1661 C.E.
8	Har K'ishan	died 1664 C.E.
9	Teg Bahadur	died 1675 C.E.
10	Gobind Singh	died 1708 C.E.

Angad made a collection of Nanak's hymns, which differed from the devotional hymns of Hinduism and Islam in that they were in the everyday language of the people, Punjabi. Hinduism still used the ancient language of Sanskrit, and Islam used Arabic. In order to write the hymns down, Angad devised a new script, called Gurmurki.

This collection of the hymns of Nanak became the foundation of the Sikh scriptures. They were full of praise for God, the one Truth:

"If I knew God as he really is
What words could I find to speak this knowledge,
Enlightened by God, the Guru has solved one mystery:
'There is but one Truth, one Giver of life;
May I never forget him.' "

The third Guru, Amar Das, began the tradition of the *langar*, or communal meal, which is still part of Sikhism today. Amar Das also worked hard to stop the Hindu custom of *sati*, in which a widow was expected to throw herself on to her husband's funeral pyre.

The fourth Guru, Ram Das, began building the city of Amritsar and the famous Golden Temple there, which was completed by Arjan, his successor. Ram Das also sent Sikh missionaries to many parts of India.

An Indian painting of sati

FOR DISCUSSION

1 Why do you think Angad wrote down the hymns of Nanak in the everyday language of the people?

2 The Sikh communal meal, the langar, emphasised the equality of all Sikhs, whatever their caste. Why was this unusual in India?

3 Why do you think Amar Das was opposed to the practice of sati? Why do you think Hindus used to do this?

The Golden Temple at Amritsar

45   Arjan and the Golden Temple

The fifth Guru, Arjan, succeeded Ram Das in 1581 C.E. He proved to be one of the most energetic and determined of all the Sikh leaders. He completed the building of Amritsar and the Golden Temple, which he called *Harmandir*, the House of the Lord. Arjan set the Golden Temple in the middle of an artificial lake, and encouraged the practice of bathing before worship.

Arjan also collected together the hymns of Nanak and other notable Gurus, including Kabir, who was a Muslim, and Jaidev, a Hindu. Arjan himself was a renowned poet, and he added some 2000 of his own verses to this collection, which was bound together and called the *Adi Granth* (First Collection).

This is one of Arjan's verses:

"Of all Religions this is the best Religion,
To speak the Holy Name with love, and to do good deeds."

Amar Das, Ram Das and Arjan lived under the Moghul (Muslim) Emperor Akbar (1555-1605 C.E.), who had married a Hindu princess and was very interested in religious reforms. Akbar is said to have visited Amar Das and taken part in the communal meal. He arranged a series of discussions between Muslims, Jains, Sikhs, Hindus, Parsees and Christians, and in 1582 published his own combination of these faiths called "Divine Faith". This never became a living religion, but it is evidence of the religious tolerance of his reign.

Akbar's son, Jahangir (1605-1627), had none of his father's tolerance and broad-mindedness. He returned to a policy of persecuting non-Muslims, and wanted to find a way of suppressing the Sikhs. Arjan was implicated in a plot to overthrow Jahangir, and was thrown into prison in Lahore and tortured to death in 1606 C.E. Arjan was the first Sikh martyr.

FOR DISCUSSION

1 Why do you think Arjan included in the Adi Granth the hymns of Muslim and Hindu poets, as well as those of Sikh gurus?

2 Why do you suppose the "Divine Faith" of the Moghul Emperor Akbar never became a living religion like Sikhism?

3 Why do you think Jahangir had Arjan killed? Can you think of any modern parallels? Do you think the killing of their leader would have had the effect of suppressing the Sikhs, or the opposite?

Guru Hargobind

Sikhs carrying on the fight to resist the Moghuls

46 Hargobind and the growth of Sikh resistance

Arjan was succeeded by his son Hargobind, who was only eleven when he took over the leadership of the Sikh community. During the forty years of Hargobind's leadership, there was intermittent fighting between the Sikhs and the armies of Jahangir and his successor, Shah Jahan. The Sikh soldiers were no match for the Government armies, but they took to the hills and developed the art of guerrilla warfare.

The oppression by the Moghuls and Hargobind's inspired military leadership succeeded in uniting the Sikhs against the Muslims. The Sikh community became increasingly nationalistic, and under Hargobind the Sikhs became a well-organised and purposeful people. This continued under the seventh and eighth Gurus; Har Rai's seventeen years of leadership were fairly uneventful, and Har K'ishan, a mere child of five when he became Guru in 1661 C.E., died of smallpox after only three years.

The ninth Guru, Teg Bahadur, fell foul of the Moghul Emperor Aurangzeb, who in 1669 C.E. issued an edict suppressing the religious freedom of all non-Muslims, including the Sikhs. Teg Bahadur ordered the Sikhs to resist; he was arrested on the charge of sedition and beheaded in Delhi in 1675 C.E.

Teg Bahadur was the youngest son of Guru Hargobind. He was a strong leader, being both a poet who wrote hymns and a soldier who led the fight against the Moghuls. He became the second martyr-Guru of the Sikhs.

The scene was now set for the final transformation of the Sikhs from the passive, meditative community begun by Nanak into a determined, nationalistic warrior race. This took place under the tenth Guru, Gobind Singh.

FOR DISCUSSION

1 Why do you suppose Hargobind's fighting men took up guerrilla warfare? Can you think of any modern parallels? Why do you think the Moghul Emperors were so keen to suppress the Sikhs?

2 Why do you think Teg Bahadur ordered the Sikhs to resist Aurangzeb?

Guru Gobind Singh

47 Gobind Singh and the formation of the Khalsa

Teg Bahadur was succeeded in 1675 C.E. by Guru Gobind Rai, his son. On the occasion of the Baisakhi celebrations, the April Harvest Festival, in 1699 C.E., Gobind Rai called together a gathering of Sikhs from all over India. When everyone had arrived and sat down, Guru Gobind Rai emerged from his tent and stood on a dais in front of the gathering with a drawn sword.

116

"My faithful Sikhs," the Guru cried. "Is there anyone here who would not lay down his life for his beliefs? I want the head of a Sikh. I must have a sacrifice!"

There was a murmur of astonishment, but no response. The Guru repeated his challenge, and again no one moved. At the third call, a man called Daya Ram stepped forward and bowed to the Guru.

"My Lord," he said. "My head is yours, to dispose of as you will."

Gobind Rai led him into the tent. The assembled Sikhs rose to their feet expectantly. There was a swish, a thud, and those nearest the tent saw a stream of blood coming from under the canvas.

The Guru emerged with his sword dripping with fresh blood. He held it aloft, and shouted, "I want another head!"

At this, many people began to shrink away. But one man stood up and came forward, and was led into the tent. Again came the swish and thud, and once more blood flowed.

The Guru came out again with the same demand, and one by one, three more Sikhs came forward. Five brave Sikhs had faced the Guru's supreme test. Then a remarkable thing happened. Before the eyes of the astonished assembly, the Guru came out of the tent — accompanied by the same five Sikhs! They were wearing new uniforms, and glowing with new confidence.

The Guru, helped by the five, prepared an iron pot of *amrit*, a nectar made from sugar cakes and water, stirred with a *khanda*, a double-edged dagger. Gobind Rai then gave some of the amrit to each of the five disciples; in this way he declared them all equal.

The five were given a new surname, *Singh*, meaning "lion". The Guru himself received amrit from the five, and took the name *Guru Gobind Singh*. This was the foundation of the *Khalsa* — the Community of the Pure, a brotherhood of soldier-saints.

FOR DISCUSSION

1   Some say that Gobind Singh actually sacrificed five goats. What do you think? Does it matter, so long as the Sikhs who were present thought that they were being asked to lay down their lives?

2   The five Sikhs were all from different castes, yet they all drank from the same bowl. What does this ritual signify? Why is this especially significant to Indians?

A Sikh with a turban and the traditional uncut beard

48   The Symbols of the Khalsa

As signs of their membership, Sikhs who have been initiated into the Khalsa wear or carry five symbols, known as the five Ks:

1 *Kesh*: Uncut hair and beard.

2 *Kangha*: Comb, to keep the hair together in a "topknot". The long hair reminds the Sikhs that they are saints as well as soldiers.

3 *Kachka*: Knee-length short trousers, much more practical for fighting men than the traditional Indian *dhoti* (loincloth). We get the word "khaki" from this.

4 *Kara*: A steel bracelet, worn on the right wrist.

5 *Kirpan*: The curved sword. This is sometimes replaced by the khanda, or dagger.

Probably, all five of these symbols originally had a military purpose; perhaps the long hair, gathered up in steel rings, acted as a helmet. The members of the Khalsa also agreed to obey four rules:

1 Not to cut their hair or beard;
2 Not to use tobacco or alcohol;
3 Not to eat the meat of any animal slaughtered in the Muslim way of bleeding to death;
4 Not to have anything to do with Muslim women, and to be faithful in marriage.

The turban is not one of the five Ks, but it was a convenient way of covering the long hair and "topknot" and it became part of the uniform of the Khalsa.

The members of the Khalsa soon had to test their fighting mettle, and the rest of Gobind Singh's life was spent in conflict. In 1704 C.E. his headquarters at Anandpur were captured by the Moghul Emperor Aurangzeb, but Gobind Singh escaped. He was eventually assassinated by a Muslim fanatic in 1708 C.E.

During most of the eighteenth century, the Sikhs were divided and without an overall leader, but unity returned in the nineteenth century under the leadership of Ranjit Singh, who succeeded in establishing a Sikh kingdom which covered virtually the whole of the Punjab. During his last years, Ranjit's main opponents were not native rulers but the British, who were pushing into north-west India. After Ranjit's death in 1839 C.E., his kingdom became part of British India, and the Sikhs became valuable allies of the British throughout the Empire. There are about 250 000 Sikhs in Britain today.

FOR DISCUSSION

1 Discuss the five symbols of the Khalsa. Do you think they all had military significance originally? If so, how?

2 Why do you think Gobind Singh stressed that the members of the Khalsa should be both soldiers and saints?

3 How do Sikhs wear or carry the five Ks today, particularly in Western countries?

The Guru Granth Sahib in a Gurdwara

49   The Guru Granth Sahib

Guru Gobind Singh ordered a revision of the collection of hymns made by Arjan, the Adi Granth, and added to it the hymns of his father, Teg Bahadur.

Guru Gobind Singh did not nominate anyone to succeed him after his death, but instead decreed in 1708 C.E. that the Sikh scripture should be given the status of Guru. From then on, the Adi Granth was known as the *Guru Granth Sahib*. *Granth* means collection, and *Sahib* means Lord or Master.

All copies of the Guru Granth Sahib are identical, no matter where they are to be found. Each one will have 1430 pages and contain 3384 hymns, divided into 15 575 verses. Each section of the Guru Granth begins with the Mool Mantra. The Granth is divided into sections, according to the author's name. Nanak's hymns come first, then those of the other Gurus, and finally the hymns of Kabir and other non-Sikh poets. Nearly 1000 of the hymns are by non-Sikhs. The *shabads* (hymns) are set to thirty-one different melodies, called *ragas*.

The key to the Sikh scriptures is said by Sikhs to be the *Japji*, written by Guru Nanak towards the end of his life. This is in the first section of the Guru Granth, after the Mool Mantra. Japji means

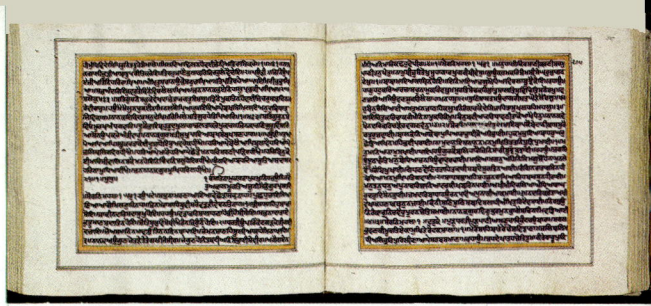

An opening of the Guru Granth Sahib

"recitation", and this is the only hymn in the Granth that is recited, not sung. It takes twenty-five minutes to recite. Here is a small part of it:

"So pure is God's name,
Whoever obeys God knows the pleasure of it in his own heart.
When the hands and feet are covered in dirt,
You remove it by washing with water.
When the clothes are dirty,
You clean them by washing with soap.
So when the mind is defiled by sin,
It is cleansed by the love of God's Name."

The Guru Granth Sahib contains the whole of Sikh belief. It stresses that there is one God, who is Truth. It echoes the Hindu belief in a cycle of rebirth, with the form of the next birth being determined by karma (good deeds). Salvation is obtained by meditating upon God, repeating his name, and serving other people. God helps in this quest for salvation, first through the ten Gurus and now through the Guru Granth Sahib.

The Guru Granth Sahib opposes the Hindu belief in caste and asserts that everyone is of equal worth. It teaches how people ought to live together; they should work honestly, worship regularly in the gurdwara, and give one-tenth of their income to charity. If a Sikh can keep these three vows, he or she will be reborn as a human, on earth. To the Sikh, this is the highest form of existence.

FOR DISCUSSION

1 Why do you think Guru Gobind Singh did not nominate a human successor, but instead nominated the Adi Granth as Guru?

2 Why do you think it is important to Sikhs that all copies of the Guru Granth Sahib should be identical?

3 How does the Sikh attitude to the Guru Granth Sahib compare with, say, the Muslim view of the Qur'an?

The Granthi reading the Guru Granth Sahib inside the Golden Temple

50   The Guru Granth Sahib and the Gurdwara

The Guru Granth Sahib is kept in a *gurdwara* (House of the Guru). A gurdwara may be any kind of building — old or new, purpose-built or converted, beautiful or plain. It will usually have outside it a flag-pole with a yellow triangular flag showing the Sikh symbols in three parts: the *khanda* (two-edged dagger), a *chakar* (circle), and two *kirpans* (curved swords).

Inside the gurdwara, everything focuses on the Guru Granth Sahib, which during the daytime is usually kept on a stool, called the *Manji Sahib*, on a raised platform, the *takht*, under a decorated canopy, the *palki*. During worship, the reader, the *granthi*, sits behind the Guru Granth Sahib to read, holding a whisk, the *chauri*, which is waved over the Guru Granth Sahib as a sign of respect. The chauri is usually made of yak hairs set into a wooden or silver holder.

Sikhs behave towards the Guru Granth Sahib exactly as if it were a living Guru. On entering or leaving, they will place their hands together and bow towards it. At night, the Guru Granth Sahib is carried respectfully to a separate room, where it is often kept on a bed.

There are no statues or idols inside a gurdwara, although on the walls there are often pictures of the ten Gurus and famous incidents in Sikh history. The gurdwara is, literally, a place where the Guru Granth Sahib is kept, and it is a meeting-place for communal worship. This is emphasised by the fact that all gurdwaras have a free kitchen, the *Guru ka langar*, where everyone who attends is expected to stay for the communal meal.

Very few Sikh homes possess a copy of the Guru Granth Sahib. The elaborate procedure of treating it like a living person, including giving it a separate room, would make this difficult in an ordinary house. Instead, most Sikhs possess a *gutka*, a small book of eighteen of the hymns from the Guru Granth Sahib.

One other collection of writings is held in high esteem by the Sikhs. This is the *Dasam Granth* — the book of the tenth Guru. It contains hymns, meditations and stories, believed to have been written by Guru Gobind Singh. The Dasam Granth was put together in 1734 by Bhai Mani Singh, a close disciple of the tenth Guru.

FOR DISCUSSION

1 Why do Sikhs treat the Guru Granth Sahib as if it were a living Guru?

2 Why is the Guru ka langar an important part of a gurdwara?

3 Why would it be unusual to find a copy of the Guru Granth Sahib in a Sikh home?

Things to do — Sikhism

1   Read the Mool Mantra (Unit 42) and the opening words of the Fourth Gospel in the New Testament (John 1, verses 1-5). Write down the similarities and differences between these two passages.

2   Imagine you are living in an Indian village in the year 1500 C.E. One day, two wandering gurus, Nanak and Mardana, arrive. At first you think Nanak is a kind of clown, with his mixture of Hindu and Muslim clothes, and you do not take him seriously. Then you begin to listen to Nanak's hymns and Mardana's music. Write a letter to a friend, describing how this experience changed your life.

3   In Unit 43 there is an account of Nanak throwing Ganges water towards his home village in the Punjab, gently mocking the Hindu practice of throwing the water to their ancestors. Working in small groups, dramatise this incident. You could pick out the best features of the individual group dramas and put them together as a class assembly, with bystanders, Hindus bathing in the Ganges, and Nanak and his followers.

4   Hold a class debate which is a reconstruction of one of the debates held by the Moghul Emperor Akbar between Muslims, Jains, Sikhs, Hindus and Christians. If you have several "representatives" of each religion, the whole class can take part. You will need to decide beforehand how the debate is to be organised; perhaps Akbar will decide on one topic to be debated, such as Life after Death, or belief in God.

5   Working as a class, dramatise the events of Baisakhi in 1699 C.E. which resulted in the formation of the Khalsa.

6   Draw a picture of an eighteenth-century Sikh warrior, showing the five Ks — Kesh, Kangha, Kachka, Kara, Kirpan.

7   The Qur'an teaches that the slave is equal to his master, and the Guru Granth Sahib asserts that all people are of equal worth, whatever their caste. Write an essay comparing these two statements, and explaining why each was so revolutionary in its time.

For Further Reading

General

Eight Major Religions in Britain: *Jane Bradshaw*. Edward Arnold.

The Religious Dimension — Holy Books: *Robin Davies*. Longman.

A Book of World Religions: *E. G. Parrinder*. Hulton.

The Many Faces of Religion: *Dicks, Merrill and Santor*. Ginn & Co.

The Sacred Writings of the World's Great Religions: ed. *S. E. Frost Jr.* McGraw-Hill.

Religions of the World: *John Ferguson*. Lutterworth.

Five Religions in the Twentieth Century: *W. Owen Cole*. Hulton.

Comparative Religions — A Modern Textbook: ed. *W. Owen Cole*. Blandford Press.

Paths of Faith: *John A. Hutchison*. McGraw-Hill.

Gods and Men — Myths and Legends from the World's Religions: *Bailey, McLeish and Spearman*. Oxford University Press.

Many Lights: ed. *D. Butler*. Chapman.

Words in World Religions: *P. D. Bishop*. SCM Press.

Hinduism

Hindu Religion, Customs and Manners: *P. Thomas*. D. B. Taraporevala Sons & Co. (obtainable through Soma Books).

Thinking About Hinduism: *E. J. Sharpe*. Lutterworth.

The Ramayana: *R. K. Narayan*. Viking Press.

The Upanishads: *J. Mascaro*. Penguin.

The Bhagavad Gita: *J. Mascaro*. Penguin.

Hindu Scriptures: *R. C. Zaehner*. Dent/Everyman.

The Hindu Tradition. Argus Publications.

The Wisdom of the Forest: *E. G. Parrinder*. Sheldon.

Upanishads, Gita and Bible: *E. G. Parrinder*. Sheldon.

Hindu Myths: tr. *W. D. O'Flaherty*. Penguin.

Hinduism: *J. Hinnells and E. J. Sharpe*. Routledge and Kegan Paul.

The Legend of Krishna: *N. Frith*. Sheldon.

The Ramayana: *E. Seeger*. J. M. Dent.

The Song of God — Bhagavad Gita: tr. *Swami Prabhavananda and C. Isherwood*. Mentor.

Myths and Legends of India: *V. Ions*. Hamlyn.

The Ramayana and the Mahabharata: *R. C. Dutt*. Everyman's Library (Dent).

Buddhism
Thinking About Buddhism: *David Naylor*. Lutterworth.
Buddhism: *T. O. Ling*. Ward Lock.
Buddhist Scriptures: *E. Conze*. Penguin.
What The Buddha Taught: *W. Rahula*. Gordon Fraser.
The Buddha: *T. O. Ling*. London.
The Story of the Buddha: *Association of Buddhist Women*. London Buddhist Vihara.
Gotama the Indian Prince: *B. Evans*. Galliard.
Some Sayings of the Buddha: *F. L. Woodward*. Oxford University Press.

Judaism
Understanding Your Jewish Neighbour: *Myer Domnitz*. Lutterworth.
The World of Jewish Faith: *Myer Domnitz*. Longman.
A Jewish Family in Britain: *V. Barnett*. R.M.E.P.
Stories from the Old Testament: *J. R. Bailey*. Beaver Books (Hutchinson).
The Jewish World: *D. Charing*. MacDonald.
Introduction to Judaism: *I. Fishman*. Valentine-Mitchell.
Everyman's Talmud: *A. Cohen*. Dent.

Christianity
Early Christian Writings: *Schools Council* (Journeys into Religion series). Granada.
Stories from the New Testament: *J. R. Bailey*. Beaver Books (Hutchinson).
The Christian Faith and Its Symbols: *J. Thompson*. Edward Arnold.
Thinking About Christianity: *R. St. L. Broadberry*. Lutterworth.
Christianity: *G. Turner*. Edward Arnold.
Christianity in Action Today: *D. D. Pringle*. Schofield & Sims.
What Do We Know About Jesus?: *L. G. Brandon*. Edward Arnold.

Islam
The Religious Dimension — Islam: *R. El Droubie and E. Hulmes*. Longman.
Islam: *Schools Council* (Journeys into Religion series). Granada.
The Way of the Muslim: *Muhammad Iqbal*. Hulton.
The Qur'an — Basic Teachings. Islamic Foundation, Leicester.
Muhammad, Prophet and Statesman: *W. M. Watt*. Oxford University Press.

Thinking About Islam: *John B. Taylor*. Lutterworth.
Muhammad The Arab Boy: *B. Evans*. Galliard.
The Meaning of the Glorious Koran: tr. *M. M. Pickthall*. Mentor.

Sikhism

Understanding Your Sikh Neighbour: *P. Singh Sambhi*.
    Lutterworth.
Sikhism: *W. Owen Cole and P. Singh Sambhi*. Ward Lock.
Thinking About Sikhism: *W. Owen Cole*. Lutterworth.
The Way of the Sikh: *W. H. McLeod*. Hulton.
Selections from the Holy Granth: *G. S. Talib*. Vikas, India
    (obtainable through Soma Books).
The Sacred Writings of the Sikhs: *UNESCO*. George Allen &
    Unwin Ltd.

Religion in Life is a series of five books:

1. Religious Buildings and Festivals
2. Founders, Prophets and Sacred Books
3. Worship, Ceremonial and Rites of Passage
4. Religious Leaders and Places of Pilgrimage Today
5. Religious Beliefs and Moral Codes

Other books by John Bailey:

Blueprint, Volumes 1–4. (Reference books for Secondary School Assemblies and R.E.) Pub. Galliard, 1976.

Gods and Men. (Myths and legends from the world's religions.) With K. McLeish and D. Spearman. Pub. OUP, 1981.

Themework. (Assembly material for Junior, Middle and Lower Secondary Schools.) Pub. Stainer and Bell, 1981.

Stories from the Old Testament. Pub. Beaver Books, 1982.

Stories from the New Testament. Pub. Beaver Books, 1982.